THE ORAL HISTORY PROJECT
Connecting Students to Their Community, Grades 4–8

Diane Skiffington Dickson,
Dick Heyler,
Linda Reilly,
Stephanie Romano

Dover Memorial Library
Gardner-Webb University
P.O. Box 836
Boiling Springs, N.C. 28017

HEINEMANN
Portsmouth, NH

Heinemann
A division of Reed Elsevier Inc.
361 Hanover Street
Portsmouth, NH 03801–3912
www.heinemann.com

Offices and agents throughout the world

© 2006 by Diane Skiffington Dickson, Dick Heyler, Linda G. Reilly, and Stephanie Romano

All rights reserved. No part of this book may be reproduced in any form or by any electronic or mechanical means, including information storage and retrieval systems, without permission in writing from the publisher, except by a reviewer, who may quote brief passages in a review.

The author and publisher wish to thank those who have generously given permission to reprint borrowed material:

Appendix 4–B, Feature Article Rubric: Copyright © Barat Education Foundation. Distributed through the American Memory Initiative of Barat Education Foundation, *www.americanmemory.org*. Reprinted by permission.

Library of Congress Cataloging-in-Publication Data
The oral history project : connecting students to their community, grades 4–8 / Diane Skiffington Dickson, . . . [et al.].
    p. cm.
  Includes bibliographical references.
  ISBN-13: 978-0-325-00853-0
  ISBN-10: 0-325-00853-1
  1. Local history—Study and teaching. 2. Oral history—Study and teaching. 3. Oral history—Methodology. I. Dickson, Diane Skiffington.
    LB1581.O73   2006
    372.89—dc22   2006022672

Editor: Danny Miller
Production editor: Sonja S. Chapman
Cover design: Jenny Jensen Greenleaf
Compositor: Valerie Levy, Drawing Board Studios
Manufacturing: Steve Bernier

Printed in the United States of America on acid-free paper
10 09 08 07 06 VP 1 2 3 4 5

Dr. Jean Winsand

This book is dedicated to Dr. Jean Winsand of the University of Pittsburgh. Jean lived for her students, from her beginnings as an elementary school teacher through her professorship at the university level. She was exemplary in so many ways—she lived life to the fullest as a wife, mother, friend, and educator. A consummate example of "walk the walk," she was ever the learner and innovator. Jean was a member of the original steering committee that put together this process for using oral history as a way to integrate and authenticate the teaching and learning of the language arts. She had, and still exerts, a profound effect on the authors of this text. No one who met her came away unaffected—she influenced them in so many ways, the most important of which was the resolve to be lifelong learners.

Jean died in 2001; until her last day, she was reading dissertations, advising students and colleagues, and doing the final editing on the Pennsylvania Literacy Framework, her last and best gift to the education community.

—Diane Skiffington Dickson

Contents

Acknowledgments vii
Foreword by Donald H. Graves ix
Introduction 1

1 Interview 11
2 Artifacts 36
3 Research 47
4 Feature Article 65
5 Memoir 88
6 Portrait 115
7 Presentation 130

Bibliography 149

Acknowledgments

The Oral History Project delineated in this book is truly the result of a cooperative and collaborative effort on the part of many educators. The seed was planted when the Governor of Pennsylvania, in an effort to ensure that standards in language arts were backed up with meaningful, in-depth, professional development, provided the resources to bring educators together for a weeklong institute. One of the aims of that experience was that classroom teachers at all levels would return to their schools able to share the model in their buildings, districts, and beyond. This book and its accompanying CD-ROM share that model with a wider audience.

The experience and creativity of the following people made this project possible:

The Original Steering Committee*

Jill Sunday Bartoli, Ph D.	Elizabethtown College, Elizabthtown, PA
Richard Brickly	Montgomery County Intermediate Unit, Norristown, PA
Diane Skiffington Dickson	Pennsylvania Department of Education, Harrisburg, PA
Marion Dugan, Ed.D.	Souderton Area School District, Souderton, PA
Bradley Gottfried	Montgomery County Community College, Pottstown, PA
Thomas Graves, Ph.D.	Folklife Consultant, Orwigsburg, PA
Stephanie Romano, Ed.D.	Stroudsburg Area School District, Stroudsburg, PA
Susan Spadafore	Pennsylvania Department of Education, Harrisburg, PA
Jean Winsand, Ph.D.	University of Pittsburgh, Pittsburgh, PA

*The positions listed are those that the members held at that time.

Staff of the Governor's Institute for English Language Arts Education

Jill Sunday Bartoli, Ph.D.	Elizabethtown College, Elizabethtown, PA
Sam Bidleman	Bloomsburg Area School District, Bloomsburg, PA
Diane Skiffington Dickson	Pennsylvania Department of Education, Harrisburg, PA
Marion Dugan, Ed.D.	Souderton Area School District, Souderton, PA
Thomas Graves, Ph.D.	Folklife Consultant, Orwigsburg, PA
Dick Heyler	Athens Area School District, Athens, PA
Linda Reilly	Huntingdon Area School District, Huntingdon, PA
Jamilla Rice	Northside Urban Pathways Charter School, Pittsburgh, PA
Stephanie Romano, Ed.D.	Stroudsburg Area School District, Stroudsburg, PA
Susan Spadafore	Pennsylvania Department of Education, Harrisburg, PA
Jean Winsand, Ph.D.	University of Pittsburgh, Pittsburgh, PA

Key Contributors

Beth Cornell	Pennsylvania Department of Education, Harrisburg, PA
Charles Hardy III, Ph.D.	West Chester University, West Chester, PA
John Gee, Thomas Salpino, and Douglas Ulkins	Athens Area School District, Athens, PA

Special thanks to the following students at East Stroudsburg University: Danielle Bevilacqua, Jennifer Bozzuto, Alexandria Gibb, Melissa St. Romaine, Stacy Sharek, Lynn Ward, Karima Woodyard who proofread and helped format the text, references, and photographs. Special thanks also to all the teachers and students (K–16) who, having experienced the process of this Oral History Project in their classrooms, have shared their stories and photographs. And a very special thanks to Danny Miller, acquisition editor at Heinemann, who saw this manuscript through from conception to a published text. Thanks to Rick Green who was the "final eyes" of the manuscript.

Foreword

by Donald H. Graves

The Oral History Project is a timely publication. At a moment when fill-in-the-blank exercises, short-answer assessments, and left-brain thinking is the vogue, *The Oral History Project* says, "Wait a minute, what about long thinking and right-brain activity?" Its authors skillfully show how long-thinking skills can be developed through interviews of older, experienced members of the community.

Some ask, "Will students sustain an effort that may take weeks or months?" This book says, "Yes, they will. Further, they will learn what it means to penetrate a subject, get under the surface, and above all, meet members of their community whom they walk by every day on the street."

The Oral History Project by Diane Skiffington Dickson, Dick Heyler, Linda G. Reilly, and Stephanie Romano describes students working to produce a tryptych for class, writing short reports, and sometimes creating much longer works. A diagram at the end of the book shows how students' writing can progress at all age levels from a two-page report to a much lengthier piece. The book documents how students systematically do background work, record interviews, take notes, and finally make presentations to teachers, classmates, and parents. (A CD-ROM accompanies the book, and the text includes disk icons in the margins so teachers can easily reference the CD to see various kinds of instruction in action.) Gradually, as students work through the details of gathering data, patterns begin to emerge. Some students do background work before the interviews and others afterward.

And the students' interviewing skills improve dramatically, which is a fact worth pondering. I have found that interviewing, the ability to gather information from others, or close in on a key fact, is a lifelong skill that has application on any job the student may acquire, and it is a skill highlighted in this book, as the students learn to refine their broad, opening queries into focused, penetrating questions that yield rich responses and a wealth of evocative information.

What the authors have done is to stitch together relationships between students and community members. After the first year of the program, community involvement builds as parents and other community members begin to anticipate results.

On the other hand, there are always surprises as each community discovers pieces of its own heritage, such as the craft and skills embodied in individuals' handiworks; the deep knowledge of historical experience, such as that possessed by war veterans; and the culture of bygone eras to be found in artifacts like recipes, old bottles, and photos.

The Oral History Project offers a way to connect classroom learning with the universe beyond school walls. Students learn to look forward to their next connection with community members. As they anticipate and pursue these interactions, they grow toward becoming lifelong learners. Research shows that students who are accomplished learners go on to achieve great things in college and community. Can there be any more valuable pursuit?

— Donald H. Graves

ntroduction

Think about an experience you have had that was important to you. Take a few minutes to freewrite about that experience.

A Pennsylvania miner recounts his experiences working in the Somerset Coal Mine; a postal worker reminiscences about some letters she delivered that were of special significance to the mayor of New York; a commercial pilot shares her log of her interesting but frightening trip to Australia; a retired veteran painfully relives his saga as he shares his medals and photographs that recapture the Vietnam War. Everyone has a story to tell. Learning about peoples' lives and their times through their stories offers an exciting adventure. The memories of these journeys have been documented by thousands of students using the Oral History Project.

The Oral History Project

The Oral History Project is a process where students interview and research the history and interests of another person. It is an authentic experience that usually involves intergenerational dialogue. These conversations get students in touch with the past while they listen, record, and explore another person's unique life story. During the process the students will be actively engaged to complete the following components.

- an interview to obtain and record the person's oral history
- research, through traditional methods and the Internet, to augment one's knowledge base while gathering the information
- artifacts to help both the interviewer and interviewee with connections and reflections
- a feature article to share the person's oral history in print
- a personal memoir written in the first person's voice to recount an important life story

- a photograph of the person to provide a visual to the project
- the presentation to share the information gathered during the project

The product can be assembled in many forms. One popular model is the triptych, a presentation board that folds into three parts. This display includes the artifacts collected during the interview and research process as well as the photos, memoir, and feature article of the person [Figure I–1].

As a culminating activity, the students may orally present their work to their peers and community members. The students feel ownership and are proud of their subjects and what they have learned through their stories. As the information from all the students is presented, the students become connected to many valuable members of the community and school. In addition, the community members marvel at the quality of the students' work and are genuinely interested in the learning experience.

The Oral History Project creates a positive impact on a personal, school, and community level. It is an enriching and transformational project through which the students obtain and practice skills necessary to enhance literacy. It has been featured in many local newspapers for its authentic learning experiences and has received The Crystal Award in 2001, cited for being an "educational program/activity that built around active engagement of parents, families, and/

Figure I–1 Assembled triptych.

or the community in school efforts that strengthen or enhance student performance and school success" (Colonial Alliance for Public Schools 2001).

The Oral History Project was purposefully designed to meet academic standards for reading, writing, speaking, and listening. During the interview, speaking and listening standards are addressed; during the writing of the memoir and feature article, types and quality of writing are taught; and during the research process, learning to read independently, to read critically in the content areas, and to analyze and interpret information are essential. Technology is incorporated through the use of the Internet for research as well as the digital camera for the photographs of the participants. School districts that have utilized the Oral History Project over a period of five years, such as the Athens Area School District in Pennsylvania, have seen significant increases in their students' reading and writing scores on the state assessments. One of many contributing factors, the Oral History Project provides students with authentic reading and writing strategies that positively influence students' achievement.

The model for the Oral History Project described in this text was initiated by the Pennsylvania Department of Education in 1998 with the Governor's Institute for English Language Arts Educators in Pennsylvania. During the initial weeklong workshop of professional development, teachers were actively engaged in the Oral History Project. They interviewed and learned about each other, used artifacts to share their stories and to write their own memoirs, researched each other's pasts, composed feature articles about their partners, and created digital portraits of each other. The resulting products were displayed on a triptych and presented to both the subject and group as a culmination of their learning experiences.

Hundreds of teachers attended the professional development institutes that were given during the next four consecutive years where they learned to teach the Oral History Project in their classrooms. In addition, hundreds of others have attended workshops presented in their local districts, in graduate reading classes, through distance learning, and at national conventions. In their own classrooms, teachers have modified the process to fit their students' grade levels, interests, and subject areas. The Oral History Project has been used successfully in all grades and in various subjects from preschool through college across the United States, Great Britain, and Australia.

During the Oral History Project, the students are interacting with an older family or community member, and the learning process consists of authentic, firsthand experiences. Students feel valued because the elders are sharing their time and knowledge. The adults feel valued as well because they have unique stories to tell and the Oral History Project provides the unique venue to share them. Relationships develop that benefit students, adults, and the community. "Researchers have learned that stories told by seniors are more interesting than similar stories told by young people, perhaps because older people have more time, more experiences, and more practice" (Miele 2002).

Although there are many variations of the Oral History Project, one format used in many classrooms has students interviewing people who are at least 40 years older than they are. In some classes, students interview each other as a way to get to know and build a community of respect for each other at the beginning of the school year. One social studies class used the project on a content and personal level where a student assumed the identity of the explorer Marco Polo and researched the life of this historical figure. This student was then paired with another student who interviewed "Marco Polo" to do an Oral History Project on this "brought to life" historical figure. A ninth-grade English class chose a piece of literature, read it, and then chose a character from the novel. Each student completed a triptych and created an original poem about some aspect of the character. Some high school classes have created Web-based Oral History Projects for the world to see.

When students present the information they have learned at an oral history gathering, the whole community shares in the learning experience. The students have become a community of learners extending beyond the confines of their classrooms and are intrinsically motivated by the inquiry process and the people they meet. Often they are reluctant to see the project end. It becomes a transformational learning experience; the subject's narrative brings that individual's history alive to be celebrated as a vital member of the community. Throughout the process, students have asked essential and probing questions and have thought critically to find the answers. They have increased their knowledge, thought about and learned new concepts, and enriched their lives.

Graves (1999) has said that with every story, there is a wish. It is our wish that while you are reading our "story," you will find yourself and your students transformed by the Oral History Project that is implemented in your classrooms.

Purpose and Contents of the Book

This book is an interactive resource guide for intermediate teachers. The purpose is to have a repertoire of teaching techniques to use with the Oral History Project in your classroom. The Oral History Project has seven components.

Chapter Content
A chapter is given to each of the following components:

- interview—to obtain and record oral histories
- artifacts—to make personal reflections and connections
- research—to ask relevant questions and find information before the interview, to seek information recursively throughout the process, and to fill in the gaps after the interview
- feature article—to highlight the person using a particular journalistic format
- memoir—to write a slice of life that brings voice to the project
- portrait—to capture a visual image
- presentation—to assemble and share the triptych at the classroom and community level

Chapter Framework
The underlying framework in each chapter follows a teaching/learning format illustrated by the acronym IMPACT:

- Instruct—explicitly teach the component
- Model—demonstrate how to do the component
- Practice—provide many opportunities for students until they feel comfortable with the component
- Assessment—develop rubrics for or with students and give them to the students ahead of time to help them to know the expectations and focus of their work
- Connect—interrelate the components of the project to arrive at a clearer understanding of the person and the process
- Transfer—use acquired social and academic skills in new situations.

When students are struggling at any stage of the process, the teacher will repeat the IMPACT learning cycle using new and individual strategies to insure success for all students.

The Appendixes

In the appendixes, you will find reflection forms for you to use as you read the chapters. These sheets will help you to be an active participant in the learning process. In addition, individual chapters include various ways teachers have adapted the project, samples of student work, and/or additional forms. This model of the Oral History Project is flexible to fit the students' and curricular needs.

CD-ROM—An Initial Model to Guide You to Make It Your Own

Accompanying this book, you will find a CD ROM titled *Oral History Project: Grades K–16*. This disk is one state's model; it is an integration of the Oral History Project with their state standards and is an invaluable tool that gives further instruction and ideas for implementing the Oral History Project in your class. Meant for professional staff development, the CD contains textual and visual materials to guide you through the background, development, and presentation of an Oral History Project. Once uploaded in your computer, an introduction thoroughly navigates you through the project. You will find guidance and information for each of the seven components/modules—interview, artifacts, research, feature (news) article, memoir, portrait, and presentation—along with a multitude of examples in text, audio, video, and photographic forms. In the book, references are made to materials found in the main menu on the CD-ROM.

It is our hope that by using the CD-ROM to complement the instructional material found in the book, you will craft a learning experience that will transform your students, yourself, and your community. The project shown on the disk and explained in this book gives an example of how you can make it your own, following your own state's standards, the IRA/NCTE standards, your own school's standards, or any curriculum that you follow. The standards on the CD-ROM are merely one state's example of how it implemented their state standards with the project. This is an initial model for you as you begin to integrate your own standards and benchmarks that you use in your districts. You can find a reference to the Information Literacy Standards put forth by the American Association of School Librarians and content area standards (see Appendix I–A).

We have crafted this book to invite you into the oral history process itself. At the beginning of each chapter there are questions that ask you to consider your own experiences and ideas. We encourage you to conjure up your memories and give some time to reflection. By doing so, you will experience more meaningful connections to the material. Pages in the Appendixes connect to the chapters and can be used for your reflections. The CD-ROM provided is an interactive tool, as is this book. As teachers, readers, and explorers of oral history, we invite you to do what we ask of our students—that is, participate. Leave passive reading behind to become an active, engaged learner in the process. Life is a balance between story and instruction. We learn through both. We hope you enjoy our story and the journeys both you and your students will take through implementing the Oral History Project.

Appendix I—A Using Oral History Techniques to Boost Literacy Skills and Meet Content Standards

Information Literacy

Standard 1. The student who is information literate accesses information efficiently and effectively.

Standard 3. The student who is information literate uses information accurately and creatively.

Standard 9. The student who contributes positively to the learning community and to society is information literate and participates effectively in groups to pursue and generate information.

Historical Understanding

Standard 2. Understands the historical perspective.
LEVEL III (Grade: 7–8)

> 6. Knows different types of primary and secondary sources and the motives, interests, and bias expressed in them (e.g., eyewitness accounts, letters, diaries, artifacts, photos, magazine articles, newspaper accounts, hearsay).

Language Arts

Standard 4. Gathers and uses information for research purposes.
Level III (Grade: 6–8)

> 1. Gathers data for research topics from interviews (e.g., prepares and asks relevant questions, makes notes of responses, compiles responses).

Standard 8. Uses listening and speaking strategies for different purposes.
Level III (Grade: 6–8)

> 4. Listens in order to understand topic, purpose, and perspective in spoken texts (e.g., of a guest speaker, of an informational video, of a televised interview, of radio news programs).

Taken from: Judy Graves and Kathy Kerst, Presenters. (October 7, 2005). Library of Congress: www.loc.gov. American Association of School Librarians.

Appendix I–B Reflection Sheet

Introduction

What is my response to the opening thoughts and questions (*in italics*)?

What was the most valuable information that I gained personally and/or for my classroom?

What do I still need to know more about? Where could I go to get that information?

What ideas can I add to what I've already learned?

1 Interview

Figure 1–1   Janna is taping and taking notes while interviewing her grandmother, Dorna Heyler.

Think about wanting to know some information about a person that you find interesting. What would you ask? What type of questions would get you the most information? Think about the kind of questions you might want to ask to help you find out about that person. Think about structuring questions that answer the following: define, describe, explain, or tell more about . . . as a way to get the person to offer their experiences to your questions.

Student: You said you were named after your dad. Since you both have the same name, "Fred," how did you know it was you or your dad, when the name, "Fred," was called . . . how did they tell you apart in your house?

Interviewee: Well . . . actually . . . there were four of us in the house with the same name.

Student:	Really? So you mean you, the son, and your dad were not the only ones named Fred? Could you tell me more about that? I mean, how did any of you know who was being asked to come do something . . . to answer the phone, for example, if there were four of you with the same name? I mean, what did you do?
Interviewee:	Yes . . . it was pretty funny. And actually, so is the story behind it all. Do you have time to hear it?
Student:	Why, yes, of course. It sounds very interesting. Could you please tell me more about it?
Interviewee:	Well, sure. You see, we knew my grandfather's name was Fred; but because he was short, they called him "Shorty." So if someone wanted "Shorty," my grandfather would answer. Then, my dad's name was also Fred, but since he was Fred Jr., named after my grandfather, Shorty, dad was called "June" as a nickname in the pecking order, you know, for junior? Then, dad's uncle was also called Fred. Everyone called him Fred. Well, when I was born, I was named Fred, too; but they called me by my middle name, Bob. This all goes back to the larger story because when I was young, I thought they didn't want so many Freds in the house. Then I learned something funny about all these people who had the same name. When I was thirteen, my grandfather had been sick and was living with us at my parents' house. I came home and found my grandfather had died. Later at the funeral home, where my parents had to go to sign papers and take care of arrangements, it was then that we were all really taken by surprise—I mean we were all totally knocked on our keisters! Mom's mouth dropped wide open and my dad started to laugh, but here we all were, getting ready for a funeral for Shorty, my grandfather. Anyway, everyone always knew Shorty was good for laughs and he always pulled tricks on folks wherever he went, but this last trick was really his best. All these years, even though folks called him Shorty, we always thought his name was Fred; but it turned out that his name wasn't really Fred at all. His given name on his birth certificate, and therefore on his death certificate, was actually Peter Francis! So you see, neither name had anything to do with the name Fred. My dad asked Shorty's brother if he knew what was

going on. My grandfather's brother, Fred, who was always really quiet, told us that my grandfather had always liked the name Fred. So sometime in his teens, my grandfather started introducing himself as Fred to people he met. Of course, to people in town, they knew him as Shorty. So everyone knew him either as Shorty or Fred . . . but no one ever knew him as Peter Francis! So my dad's name, Fred Jr., really didn't show that dad was junior to his dad, Shorty, since Shorty's real name turned out not to be Fred at all! He was a real card, my grandfather was, and so was his brother, Fred, for not saying anything to any of us until he was asked at my grandfather's funeral.

This interview between the student (interviewer) and his grandfather (interviewee) marks the first step in the Oral History Project.

Tell Me a Story: What Is Your Favorite Story?

Everyone has a story to tell; everyone enjoys hearing a good story. Whether the story is humorous or sad, informational or inspirational, the storyteller engages the listener. Gratefully, sharing stories and experiences through the oral tradition exists because it forms an enriching and connecting part of many cultures and communities. It functions as the vital handing down of family memories and community stories—their successes and changes. It fills in the gaps that other ways of writing, reading, and talking about events do not. Being able to hear another's story can be both fulfilling and rewarding.

In the previous interview, the interviewee shares a humorous story that gives insight both to the personality of one of his relatives and to the storyteller as well. When the interviewee shares this unique experience with the interviewer about his grandfather, a connection is being spun between the two individuals. There is a trust being woven that is unique to the listener and the speaker, the interviewer and the interviewee. Because of that bond, more stories may be shared.

CD Connection

On the Main Menu screen, click on the Gallery and scroll down to Interview Module, Dr. Hardy - Preparing Questionaire Before The Interview.

As an added benefit, looking at the form of the question initially asked during the interview exemplifies that the interviewer's structure is open-ended. That is to say, the interviewee cannot possibly merely answer "yes" or "no" to the question posed by the interviewer. Questions that elicit these answers are usually dead ends to a conversation. Consider the following that demonstrates the difference between "skinny" or close-ended questions and "fat" or open-ended questions:

"Skinny" Questions

Where were you born?

Do you have a big dog?

Do you like to read?

"Fat" Questions

Describe what you wore to church, Grandma, when you were younger.

Tell me about/describe your dog.

Explain why you like mysteries.

It is the open-ended, rather than the close-ended, structure that invites the interviewee to elaborate and tell the whole story. The inquiry stimulates the opportunity for the interviewee to reply with a long answer. In addition, the response entertains and informs the interviewer, as the question's structure encourages the interviewee to tell the interviewer more information. The information given may become a cornerstone for asking additional open-ended questions that will garner opportunities for the interviewer to learn more information about his subject.

In another similarly open-ended question, a granddaughter asks, "Can you describe what you wore to church when you were young, Grandma?" The question frames a response that may lead to a fully developed, detailed response uniquely shared between two generations. The question and its answer form a connection, a conduit between the youth and elder. Telling her granddaughter that she treasured wearing her short white gloves and broad-rimmed yellow straw hat, for instance, depicts a time where it was a custom, style, and routine to wear gloves and a hat to church. In a relatively short period, both individuals experience the enjoyment of this conversation based on a question about a past experience. Notice that the interviewer uses questions that probe and that are structured to ask the interviewee to describe, explain, give details, or answer the question *why* about a situation, time, or person. How does the interviewer formulate questions that will stimulate the responses needed to understand the person being interviewed?

Speaking and Listening Activities

The student-listener needs to identify, acquire and practice important skills (see Interview Process Checklist, Appendix 1–A). Because part of being an active and effective listener involves using body language skills to show an interest in what the speaker is saying, model these skills for your students and then practice using these skills during class time. As you begin instruction, discuss with the students what body language and proxemics are within the context of an interview. For instance, when a person is speaking, students need to look at the speaker and be engaged with what is being said. Leaning forward, making eye contact, raising eyebrows, and smiling or frowning when appropriate are a few of the behaviors that need to be explained, modeled, and practiced. These body language skills help the interviewer depict proper and respectful behavior during the interview.

Following the initial discussion and modeling, students practice these body movement skills and proxemics: leaning slightly toward the speaker, making eye contact, and using facial expressions that indicate interest in what the speaker is saying. They may also practice other body language features in a variety of ways during classroom discussions. Consider trying the following examples.

CD Connection

On the Main Menu screen, click on the Gallery and scroll down to Interview Module, click on Examples of Open-Ended, Skinny/Fat Questions

1. Divide the class of students into pairs or allow the students to pick a partner to create their own pair. Tell the students to face each other, with one student playing the role of listener and the other student, the speaker. Direct the listener to offer absolutely no gestures, no verbal or nonverbal cues, and no comments or proxemics. The speaker is directed to speak nonstop about how to play a favorite game or to describe a recently seen movie.

2. After two minutes, the students switch roles. Again, the same ground rules apply, where the listener only listens, as the speaker talks nonstop about the chosen subject. In between much laughter and frustration, the students learn that not responding to a speaker is truly a difficult task and body language is an important skill to use while listening.

3. When two additional minutes pass, stop the pairs and reconvene the group. In a debriefing, discuss with the students which role was easier, to be the speaker or the listener. Students' comments are recorded on the board or an overhead.

A reflection time ensues on the way the students felt as listeners, when they could not ask questions or even smile or frown at the speaker's comments. Most suggest that they also wanted to talk or react to what was being said, at least to lean forward or even raise their eyebrows or laugh when they heard certain bits of information to which they wanted to respond.

For many of the students who commented on their role as speaker, the general view was they felt it was difficult to become involved or engaged in the topic when there was no response, not even a headshake, smile, or grunt. Many students added that it was very difficult not to interject some sort of comment in response to the speaker's statements. Some even questioned whether or not the listeners were being respectful because they offered no responses at all.

Eventually, elicit from the students specific characteristics they feel make it easier for them to listen. For example, have a class discussion that emphasizes the need for interviewers to listen carefully and respectfully. Ask the students why it is important. List their comments on the board or the overhead. Add and discuss the students' ideas, including techniques they may not mention. For example, the students should be aware that for the Oral History Project, careful listening leads to asking follow-up questions that will help them know more about the interviewee. As the students acquire more knowledge, they will gather sufficient information to conduct research to craft their feature article about the person.

Another engaging activity that you can do is to ask the students to tell each other a story on a familiar topic that they mutually enjoy. In this case, there is no other purpose to be derived except the pleasure of being told a story as they simultaneously practice being effective listeners. Encourage the students to lean toward each other, have eye contact, ask clarifying questions, and offer behaviors that characterize them as effective listeners. As the students are involved in this activity, you can circulate among the students, jotting down instances of effective listening skills that were observed to share with the entire group following the ten-minute activity.

Another important instructional activity is modeling for the students several ways to ask follow-up questions. For example, as a class, create a list of questions on the board that reflects a single subject—pets. For those students who may not have a pet, encourage them to think about a pet they would like to have or even invent their own pet. This will allow them to be part of the activity and simultaneously opens the door for some clever and outlandish creatures. Then ask a student to assist by answering the following questions to model for the class ways to form follow-up questions:

> "I have a pet, a dog named Noodles. If you have a pet, what kind of pet is it?"
>
> "Tell me how you went about naming your pet."
>
> "Explain why you chose your pet rather than any other type."
>
> "Give details about what you feed it. How often do you feed it?"
>
> "Describe what you do together." (If the pet is a fish, this question will not make any sense, but will make the students laugh.)
>
> "Describe what your pet does that makes you laugh."

Then group the students into pairs. One student asks the other student five questions about the student's pet. The students' questions are derived from the list of questions put on the board to get the students used to the process of using follow-up questions. When the list of questions is posed and the responses noted, the students then switch roles. During this activity, remind the class to practice using effective listening skills including proper body language skills and proxemics.

These simple activities and others give students the opportunity to practice their listening skills in order to become effective interviewers. It is useful to revisit these listening skills often with the students. Being a respectful, active listener is expected within the larger context of the classroom in addition to the time when they will be conducting the interview for the Oral History Project. Take a few minutes to reflect with your students, asking them what they learned about effective follow-up questions. Doing these preliminary activities with their classmates helps the students feel comfortable and unthreatened while practicing their initial interview techniques.

Through discussion with other students, they realize that the information they gathered during the interview will enable them to know more about the interviewee, which is an important point of this process.

The Interviewee Is the Central Focus

An important aspect of being an effective listener is being an interviewer who is willing to become less important than the interviewee who is telling the story. Model how the interviewer needs to focus on the interviewee. Explain to the students that if they are focusing on a written question or a future activity that will follow the interview, the student's interest will be diverted rather than on the person being interviewed. To practice respect as well as effective listening, the students need to realize the interviewee is the center of the attention. Help the students generate topic areas of interest rather than specific questions. A short list of topics encourages the students to listen to the interviewee's stories to produce appropriate follow-up questions. The student should avoid interjecting her own experiences on a topic; to do so shifts attention away from the interviewee as the central focus.

It's Not About the "Truth"

An effective listener is interested in hearing a story from the interviewee's point of view, whether it agrees or conflicts with the interviewer's perspective. Neither the granddaughter in the interview with her grandmother about what she wore to church on Sunday nor the interviewer in the initial anecdote about the all the relatives named Fred is concerned with veracity. The interview is based on the interviewee's perception about his past. It is not up to the interviewer to correct the interviewee's perception about an event, person, or anything else. The purpose of the interview is to gain information about the interviewee, including the way it is perceived and remembered. It is this verbal perspective that enriches an experience that a history book usually does not capture within its scope; it makes history come alive.

360 Degrees Later

If there are words that the interviewee uses that are unfamiliar, the interviewer should feel comfortable stopping the conversation to ask clarifying questions. Because of a developing relationship, the interviewer trusts the interviewee will reply. At the same time, the interviewer understands the pitfalls of unnecessary interruptions and avoids creating them. Ideally, the experience becomes a time of interaction, engagement, and entertainment. The student is interested in getting as much information as possible from the interviewee. As new information unfolds, the student is skilled and ready to pose follow-up questions, getting the information about the interviewee that will lead to research and eventually be used to write the feature article.

Bringing in the Elders

In a small Australian community, Tighes Hill, located in Newcastle, New South Wales, a group of ten-year-olds, with guidance from their teacher and a small group of University of Newcastle students, gathered with a group of elders from their community. Their ultimate purpose was to generate oral histories using the Oral History Project. The initial visit was for the participants to get acquainted in a safe environment. This occurred during a lovely informal tea that created a relaxed atmosphere for everyone.

During this initial visit, the elders piqued the children's interest as they each introduced themselves. The children briefly learned that some of their community's elders were carpenters, teachers, social workers, pilots, engineers, bricklayers, mothers, and fathers. They learned that many of these elders from their community emigrated from Europe to Australia either before or during World War II.

Prompted by questions posed by the children, the elders shared their time and experiences. By telling stories of their childhoods, these elders fascinated the ten-year-olds' imaginations. The experience was a meaningful event for both the students and the elders as it set the stage for the students wanting to learn more and helped the students formulate questions—some of which were follow-up and/or clarifying questions.

A Snippet of the Interview

Student: How did you feel when you were leaving your house where all your toys and dogs were?

Interviewee: Yes . . . I could not be quieted at first. I was really very, very sad . . . inconsolable, really. You see I had to leave many of my family . . . my friends . . . my house . . . my dogs . . . my pony—everything! I was so sad. For a long time I was sad. All the time we traveled I was crying. I think I cried all the way, even after we arrived in Sydney. Even though my parents kept telling me how lucky I was . . . you know, because I was alive and because we were mostly together, you know? And I knew deep down that I truly was lucky. But I was still so very, very sad. [Shared by an elder of Polish descent, as she remembered daily events during World War II that prompted their emigration.]

Student: Have you been back to where you grew up?

Interviewee: Yes. I did go back about 20 years ago. Some of the little shops were still there, and that was comforting; but of course not everything was like I remembered it to be. Still, it was good to go back . . . to visit. I was curious about whether or not there had been any changes in my neighborhood. The small corner place where my sister and I used to go for sweets after school was still there. My sister was much older than I . . . and very pretty, too. She had lots of boys who tried to get her attention. Seeing the shop made me remember some of those good moments we spent together when I went there with my sister. Sometimes we'd just talk and laugh while drinking our tea. It was lovely then.

Going Where the Interviewee Leads You

As with this exchange of ideas, elementary and young adolescent students often wonder what they would do in certain situations when listening to interviewees' responses to their questions. Later when the students have practiced and carried out their formal interviews, it is important to discuss some of the experiences they encountered, the questions and the responses that were intriguing as well as problematic or troublesome for them. Often in these discussion sessions, students come up with further questions. They write them down in their notebooks and share them with the teacher during class time set aside for conferencing. In addition, many students find it interesting and necessary to gain more information about a topic, which leads to doing informal or more formal research. For example, the students may want to go on the Internet and browse sites for World War II or simply ask questions of an older relative or family friend.

Where the Interview Takes Place

There are two basic settings from which to choose for creating a comfortable atmosphere for an interview to take place: bringing interviewees into the classroom or going to where the interviewees live. Often, the issue of keeping students safe once they are beyond the classroom walls dictates that the interviewee is either a member or a close friend of the family. A parent sometimes will accompany their child to the house but stay out of the picture while the interview is taking place. In some situations, the interview may take place over a phone or even via email, but this is a rarity. To return to the Tighes Hill example, the safety issue led to asking the community members to come to the school, so these fifth- and sixth-level students could interview them in a monitored environment. Whether the setting selected is the school or the home, both the students and the interviewees need to feel comfortable with each other before a sharing of the person's memories and stories begin. It was decided to have a tea with the elders who came to Tighes Hill School before the more formal interviews with the children that were scheduled to take place at the end of the week. In this way, the members of the community informally met each other, the children, and the teachers. The backdrop of scones, biscuits, fresh fruit, juice, and tea proved to be a good choice where everyone met and talked a bit with each other prior to the return for the actual interviews. After the tea, the elders left and the teacher reviewed the interviewing steps the students had previously learned. The students were anxious for the formal interviews to begin, even though they wanted to practice more before meeting with their particular elder at the end of the week. In total, these students and elders eventually met four times during the interview phase of this Oral History Project. In other cases and other classes, there may be only one or two interview sittings.

Figure 1–2 Mark Roccograndi interviews Mr. Angelo Polo about the hand tools he used to quarry slate at the Dally Slate Quarry.

Practicing the Interview

Getting students started with conducting an interview by modeling for them in front of the classroom with a willing student or group of students provides a useful departure point that is fun, instructive, and relaxing. You, as the teacher, are the interviewee either with one student playing the role of the interviewer or in an open forum of students asking the teacher a variety of questions. Conduct a brief interview session with the students followed by discussion about the types of questions asked by the students. Then proceed with a second interview session. The most difficult role for you throughout both sessions will be to provide *only* the answer to the students' specific questions to encourage them to ask questions that require substantial, open-ended answers. For example, in the first question and answer session, a student may ask you if you like to play sports. The answer for such a "skinny" or *closed* question is either "yes" or "no." A more effective, "fat" or *open* question directs you to talk about which sport you prefer

CD Connection

On the Main Menu screen, click on the Gallery and scroll down to Interview Module, click on Teacher Describes How She Modeled Interview - Gr.12.

to play and/or watch. Consider the following scenario that deals with closed- and open-ended questions:

Teacher: Do you have a question for me?
Student: Where were you born?
Teacher: I was born in Honolulu, Hawaii.
Student: Hawaii? And you're *here*? Can you tell me more about being here and why you're not in Hawaii any more?
Teacher: Yes. My father was in the Navy and was stationed in Hawaii. That's why I was born there and not anywhere else. We only stayed there until I was three years old, when he was shipped to another place."

Notice that in this brief interaction the student asks both an open-ended or fat question as well as a skinny or close-ended question. Both question types provide the student with information about you as the teacher. If he continues asking close-ended questions, the student will most likely be talking more than the interviewee because more questions will be needed to gain information; therefore, it will take longer to learn about the interviewee.

To refine the students' interviewing skills, interrupt the question and answer period and ask the class to identify the type or structure of questions being asked. Are they open-ended or close-ended questions? Has considerable information been gathered or are more questions still needed? Why? Through class discussion and modeling, the students realize the importance of asking open-ended questions to gain the amount of information needed from the interviewee.

Often the first round of questioning causes introspection about the type of questions being asked. Continue a second round of questioning from the class. After answering a very short number of questions for which there is only a yes or no response—for example, as with simple facts, such as date of birth—interspersed with questions that also require longer answers, pause again and ask the students to reflect on the type of questions they asked. Reflecting and discussing which type of questions are giving more information will often lead to a different, more enriched type of questioning when the interview ensues again. The students soon become aware of and can distinguish between fat and skinny question forms. They note that sometimes it is important to ask skinny questions, which yield a yes or no answer, and sometimes it is vital to ask a majority of fat questions to find out the most information about the interviewee in a shorter amount of time. The students realize the value in practicing open-ended questions, because these queries will afford them more information about the person being interviewed.

Practicing Close-Ended and Open-Ended Question Format

After close-ended and open-ended questions have been modeled, the next teaching activity guides them to ask questions about themselves. In this activity, two students take turns asking each other five questions, offering only the specific bare-bones answer to the question posed, to practice in a more deliberate way telling an open-ended from a closed-ended question structure. Then, have the students select another student. One student from each group picks a subject on a 3 x 5–inch card, such as dogs versus cats as pets, football versus soccer as a team sport, and so forth. Allow each student sufficient time to come up with five questions to ask on the subject when it is her turn to be the interviewer. While one student talks, the other takes notes on the speaker's answers. Then they reverse roles. Following approximately five to ten minutes of this activity, students volunteer to interview the person in front of the class on the subject printed on the 3 x 5–inch note card. This latter step depends on the maturity level of the students and may need modification to fit the age group. The class members share their experiences and reflect on the process and the types of questions asked.

This activity may be practiced several times during the week, until all the students can construct questions that are both in an open and closed format as well as know and understand the difference in the types of questions formed. Although it is stressed that an interviewer will get more information from an open-ended question format, it is also important the students know that close-ended questions have their place. Hence the students learn both formats are important as long as the bulk of the interview is not comprised of skinny answers, which ultimately makes the students work harder at getting information about the stories from the person they interview (see appendixes for sample questions, checklist, and assessments).

The Importance of Taping the Interview

The goal of the interview is to gain as much information from the interviewee's perspective as possible. How often have we heard information that differs from another? Being able to take notes becomes an important discussion. Many students realize they cannot always take notes in a totally accurate manner as a story unfolds during the interview.

Instruction on how to take accurate notes and its importance needs to takes place. Can the interviewer effectively listen to the interviewee and take down accurate notes at the same time? Can the interviewer accurately remember what is said without taking notes? This discussion is followed by an activity. In this activity, students are first asked about taking effective notes in general in their different subjects. What type of notes do they take in math class, in social studies, or in health class? The discussions reveal the complexity and difficulty in both listening and writing down what is being said at the same time. Everyone also agrees that it is sometimes difficult to take down in an exact manner all the information that is being given by the interviewee.

In a separate but related issue, the students agree that sometimes they do not always know what information to include in their notes. To help them understand, direct the students to take two minutes to share an experience while their partners take down the information given. After two minutes, the partners switch roles for another two-minute time period. Then lead a discussion concerning the importance of jotting down everything the speaker has to say within the allotted time. Although some students were able to take accurate notes, much of the experiences were similar to the following interaction:

> "Katey wrote down that I hiked around Rehoboth, when it was Alice Springs. I've never even been to Rehoboth before! What was she thinking?" laughed Maggie.
> "Yeah? Well you wrote down that I had two dogs and a cat, but it was two cats and a dog instead!" replied Katey.

This activity is useful in getting the students to see that sometimes their ability to take notes and listen at the same time can be enhanced by asking questions, by using their own note coding, and often by using other devices that go beyond their own skills. Students understand the purpose and importance of using the tape recorder during a formal interview for the Oral History Project. Taping the interview picks up what note taking often cannot. The audiotape will preserve the tone of voice, which may portray attitudes and emotions. There may be significant pauses. Taping the interview preserves more clearly the true interactive nature of the interview and many of its nuances. In order to maintain the flow of the conversation, take the class through the taping process. (See the Sample Summary Checklist in Appendix 1–B.)

Getting Ready for the Taping Process

Obtain a signed permission form allowing the interviewer to tape and use the taped information for the Oral History Project (see sample in the Appendix 1–C). The taping process is practiced several times during the week before giving each student a homework assignment that involves taping and writing. Although most students will be quite familiar with cassette tape recorders, important guidelines should be clearly articulated for the students to follow.

1. Practice putting in a tape and then turning it over.
2. Practice putting in the batteries properly and replacing them with fresh batteries.
3. Practice turning the tape recorder on and off, fast-forwarding it, putting it on pause and on record, and rewinding it.
4. Practice saying something on the tape and rewinding it to listen for an appropriate volume level.
5. Practice adjusting volume level and microphone placement with the subject.
6. Practice recording the interviewer's name, the interviewee's name, the place where the interview is taking place, and the date of the interview.

In addition to practicing these six simple steps to feel confident when taping the interviewee, instruction is given on the following steps when the interview commences.

1. Have extra batteries and extra tapes on hand—generally ninety-minute tapes are recommended as they are less at risk to distort than the longer tapes.
2. Set the scene for taping, so the interview is in a quiet room and is not taking place next to a phone, a crying or needy child or animal, or a television or radio that are turned on while the interview is taking place.
3. For the technical aspects of taping, the tabs at the end of each tape need to be removed so the interview is not mistakenly erased; the cassettes should be properly labeled with the correct identification on the outside case as well as on the tape itself; the quality of the recording should be observed, with a minimum of

ambient noises; and a transcription of the interview should be obtained. Transcriptions and tapes should be preserved but are not part of the Oral History Project.

Taping a Partner

The purpose of this activity is for one student to ask questions while taping his or her partner. During this short ten-minute session, the students focus on getting a feel for the equipment. They practice speaking clearly, practice getting the microphone close enough to the speaker so the information is recorded clearly at the proper volume. They practice locating and using the pause and/or stop button. Finally, they practice using open- and close-ended questions and the other effective listening skills they have learned. After ten minutes, they switch roles and repeat the activity. Both students then listen to the tape of the other partner's responses. They may need to listen to it more than once. The students then write a critique of the tape addressing what they did well and suggesting improvements that should be made during the next taping session.

Assessment

Assessing the learned skills of listening, interviewing, and tape recording is a critical part of the learning process. For the interview, there is a checklist that enables the students to know what they are to be doing and at what level of competence they are operating when conducting an interview in its various stages. In this way, the students can self-assess, easily seeing where their strengths and needs are. They can feel confident and competent as they practice the interview process and know the areas where they can improve their skills before transferring their use in the actual interview.

Interviewing is part of a transformational experience for both the interviewer and the interviewee. Recognizing that young students are truly interested in the perspective and memories of elders and actively engaged listening to their stories gives value to the student-interviewer as it honors the interviewee. Sharing the final product with the interviewee and eventually the community closes the gap between the generations to offer an experience that is rich, warm, inviting, and valuable. The students become the story keepers of the community; the torch is passed on from one generation to another. The students have collaborated with their elders to learn about the past from a unique point of view that may lead to personal research. With the interview audiotaped, other members of the interviewee's family can enjoy the elder's recollections and perspectives that characterize the interviewee's persona. In many instances, the taped interviews are catalogued and stored with proper care in a communal place to be shared with future generations and future researchers. Begun in 1975, the Ellis Island Oral History Project is an informal collection of interviews of individuals who immigrated to the United States through Ellis Island. Teachers can share a collection of these interviews from Veronica Lawlor's book *I Was Dreaming to Come to America*. More recently, begun in 2003, the StoryCorps Oral History Project is "a national initiative to instruct and inspire individuals to record oral histories and create meaningful personal experiences for the participants" (Kniffel 2005).

For more information on the interview process:

Hoopes, James. 1979. *Oral History: An Introduction for Students*. Chapel Hill, NC: The University Press.

Kniffel, Leonard. 2005. "Listening as an Act of Love." *American Libraries: The Magazine of the American Library Association*, December.

Lawlor, Veronica. 1995. *I Was Dreaming to Come to America*. New York: Viking.

Library of Congress. Website: www.loc.gov/americaslibrary.

Ritchie, Donald A. 1995. *Doing Oral History*. New York: Twayne Publishers.

Appendix 1–A The Interview Process Checklist

1. I practiced using the equipment so everything would go smoothly.
2. I brought extra batteries and tapes.
3. I tested the equipment before and after the interview to make sure all was in working order.
4. I began the tape with a general introduction to the interview that included the interviewee and interviewer's name, the location, and date.
5. I remembered that the interview is *not* a general dialogue and so I did the following:
    a. kept my questions focused on the interviewee rather than on my own personal views
    b. asked predominately open-ended questions
    c. used follow-up questions
6. I used effective eye contact.
7. I used other body language and effective listening skills such as leaning forward, nodding, smiling, and offering short phrases of understanding.
8. I did not challenge in any way any information that I thought may be inaccurate.
9. I was aware of giving respect to my interviewee at all times.
10. I did not feel compelled to fill in moments of silence, knowing that silence is an important part of the process.
11. I gave the signed release for the interview to my teacher to keep on file.
12. I kept my interview to no more than a total of ninety minutes.
13. I gave a copy of the taped interview to my interviewee.
14. I wrote a thank-you note to my interviewee after the final interview.

Appendix 1–B Sample Summary Checklist for the Interview

1. I was extremely familiar with my tape recorder before I began. I knew exactly what each button did, so I did not take up valuable time figuring it out with my interviewee.
2. I put a formal introduction on the tape. I included my name, the name of my interviewee, the day's date, and the location of the interview.
3. I asked open-ended questions.
4. I made and used an outline of topics. Even though I practiced with a list of questions with my partner, I remembered each interview is a unique exchange with a unique individual. I wanted a smooth interview.
5. I asked follow-up questions. I listened for places in the information where I wanted to know more based on where, when, and why question formats.
6. I used silence to draw out more information.
7. I did not ask any leading questions that would make my interviewee either agree or disagree with me.
8. I did not add my own opinions to any of the topics. I know this is an interview about my interviewee, rather than about me.
9. I did not argue with my interviewee about anything said.
10. I politely stopped the interview when I needed to turn over the tape or replace a battery.
11. I treated my interviewee with respect at all times.

Appendix I–C Sample Permission Form

Anywhere Area School District

Fourth-Grade Oral History Project
Interviewer/Interviewee Agreement

Thank you for participating in our Oral History Project. The information gathered from this interview will be used to enhance the students' understanding of local history. A "feature article" will be written to summarize the interview, which will be displayed along with your portrait and memoir when the final project is completed. The taped interview may be given to our local museum to become a primary source of local history documentation. If you would like a copy of this tape, simply provide a blank tape and a copy will be made and delivered to you. This is an exciting project for the students as it will serve to connect generations within our community. We greatly appreciate your willingness to be a part of this process.

Having read the above, I knowingly and voluntarily permit the Anywhere Area School District and the local museum to have full use of the information shared during this interview.

Interviewee Signature _____ Date _____

As the interviewer, I agree to be polite and courteous throughout the interview process. I will assist the interviewee through the portrait procedure and treat any artifacts with the greatest of care. I will share my completed work with the interviewee.

Interviewer Signature _____ Date _____

Teacher Signature _____

*This is a sample agreement used in a fourth-grade class and is not intended for any use beyond being a sample. Any agreements that require signatures should be reviewed with and approved by your administrator.

Adapted from the CD-ROM.

Appendix 1–D Possible Questions to Stimulate Discussion

(For specific topic areas, work together with your partner for additional questions. Please make sure to meet with me for final question suggestions and approval.)

1. When were you born?
2. In what place were you born: at home, in a hospital, other?
3. In what city or town? Country?
4. What is your nationality?
5. What do you know about your family name? Was your family name changed when your family originally came to this country? What was it? In what language?
6. Who were the first family members to settle in this country? What were their names?
7. What brought them here and what do they remember doing to finance their trip here? Was there a sponsor for any family member? Who was it? What were the conditions?
8. Where did they first arrive? What possessions did they bring with them?
9. What language did they speak and where exactly did they come from? Did the place they came from have a different name from what it is called today?
10. What stories were told about what life was like for them before they came here?
11. Where did they first settle when they came here? How did they make their living?
12. When and where were your grandparents born? What were their full names?
13. What were some of the stories or songs that your grandparents told you about where they came from or what life was like for them when they were younger?
14. Where they are buried? If they are buried in a church cemetery, does the parish have information on file that they can access to share?
15. What were the full names of your own parents?
16. When and where were they born and brought up?
17. What were your parents like? What can you tell me about your parents?
18. How did they make a living?
19. How many aunts or uncles do or did you have? What were their names? What do you remember about them?

20. Who were your favorite relatives? What made them your favorite(s)?
21. How many brothers or sisters do or did you have? What were their names and when were they born in relationship to you?
22. What were they like as young people? Talk about any special or funny stories that you remember about them.
23. Where did you live as a child? What was your home town like back then? What do you miss most about it?
24. Please tell me what life was like when you were very young and growing up. What are some of your earliest memories?
25. What did you look like? What were you like as a young child? Tell me a story to show the way you were or the way you acted.
26. If you had a nick name, how did you get it?
27. How much schooling did you have? What was your favorite subject? What subject did you dislike?
28. If you had a favorite teacher, what was he or she like? In what ways did he or she influence you?
29. If you worked as a child, what did you do? How old were you? What type of work did you do? Describe a typical working day.
30. What did you like doing most as a child? What games or instruments did you play?
31. Talk about your favorite pet or toy.
32. Who were your best friends and what did you do together?
33. What is the happiest memory in your childhood and when did it happen?
34. What was the saddest time? Can you tell me about it?
35. What was your first experience with death? What happened? What did it mean to you? How did you deal with the loss?
36. What beliefs or ideals do you think your parents tried to teach you to live your life?
37. Who do you think influenced your life the most when you were young? In what way?
38. What great person have you known in your life? What made him or her special to you?
39. What were your teenage years like?
40. What goals did you have as a young person and what goals, if any, did your family have for you?
41. If you went to college, where, and what did you study?
42. What led you to choose the type of work you do or did? What was there about it that you liked the most? The least?
43. When did you start working and what kinds of jobs were your first ones? What were they like and how did you feel you did on them?

44. When did you first meet your husband/wife? Under what circumstances?
45. What was he or she like when you first met? What attracted you to him or her? (Or did you dislike each other at first? Why?)
46. How old were you both?
47. What was your courtship like?
48. How soon after meeting did you marry?
49. What was life like in the early days of your marriage?
50. Where did you live? What was life like working at that time? What was a typical day like for you at work or home?
51. Did you go to war? Which one? Where were you stationed and what was it like? How long did you serve and in what branch? (If female, ask what difficulties did you experience as a member of the service.)
52. When did you have children? After whom was each child named?
53. When you think back to the children when they were very young, what stories come to mind about them? How did the children change your life?
54. Looking back, what do you think has been the happiest time in your life? What was the worst? How do you deal with sad moments? What helps you the most?
55. What do you think was the turning point in your life? How did your life change after this event? How did you learn to be on your own? When?
56. What have been the major accomplishments in your life?
57. What have been the biggest problems, mistakes, or difficulties in your life? How did you overcome them or what did you learn from them? How did they affect your life?
58. If you were to give advice to me, or any young adults today, what would it be? What have you learned from life? What has been its biggest surprise?
59. What do you think is the best way that we might want to conduct our lives?
60. What do you think your strengths are? What special things do you know or do of which you are proud?
61. What activities do you enjoy most: sports, music, dancing, reading, cooking, working, studying a certain subject, traveling . . . others?
62. What is the most wonderful place you visited? What is your favorite time of year or holiday?
63. If you had your life to do all over again, what would you do differently? What would you do that would be the same?
64. Are there any thoughts you'd like to add?

Linda Reilly, Language Arts and Social Studies teacher, Huntingdon Area School District

Appendix 1—E Reflection Sheet

Chapter 1: Interview

What is my response to the opening thoughts and questions (*in italics*)?

What was the most valuable information that I gained personally and/or for my classroom?

What do I still need to know more about? Where could I go to get that information?

What ideas can I add to what I've already learned?

2 Artifacts

Figure 2–1 WWII Veteran, Jack Lippincott, proudly displays his army uniform.

Think about some things that are important to you. It may be an object or event or place that holds fond memories or has special significance. It may even be a person who has influenced your life. Tell someone the story of why these are important to you.

I've been painting for quite a long time now. Let me show you some of the landscapes I've painted. I often sit at my kitchen table and look out the window overlooking the peaceful countryside. The scenery gives me the inspiration for my paintings.

—Lorraine Brong, retired community member

When I was a district magistrate, this is the gavel I used in the courtroom. One of the most interesting cases I've heard involved the abduction of a four-year-old child. When the courtroom became unruly, I used this gavel many times to maintain order.

—Henry McCool, retired District Magistrate

I have this exceptional cake recipe from my grandmother who was an immigrant from Germany. She was a cook for the clergy in Europe when she was a young girl. She taught me how to bake the Dobos Torte, a seven-layered cake with a smooth chocolate mousse filling. When I was little, she baked it for me every year on my birthday. It's the best cake there is.

—Christine Newhard, former elementary teacher

Artifacts are the vehicles that help people tell their stories. Artifacts are usually thought of as items from the person's past experiences. In addition to items, sometimes an event or even a person holds special meaning for the person being interviewed. Although these representations are abstract artifacts that cannot be seen or touched, nevertheless, they can be used to help people generate their stories. The purpose of including artifacts during the interview is to further the student's understanding of the person. Artifacts are a starting place for conversation and often become the icebreaker in the interview. It gives the interviewer a chance to ask a question about the item, event, or person, which will sometimes jog the memory of the storyteller. This puts both the interviewer and interviewee at ease.

For Lorraine Brong, a retired community member who volunteered to be interviewed for the Oral History Project, her paintings are the items that help her to tell her story. They are part of her life that is important to her and she is proud she can share them with the interviewer. They tell about her as a person today. In her eighties, she still continues to paint and will often frame her landscapes and give them to family members. Her paintings help her to understand herself and who she is. They also helped the interviewer understand her personality. In time, they will become artifacts for her relatives by which they will remember her.

CD Connection

On the Main Menu screen, click on the Gallery and scroll down to the Artifacts Module, Thoughts on the Value of Artifacts

The gavel helped Henry McCool remember his past years as a district magistrate. It is an item that evokes his memories of being in the courtroom, also an artifact for him. He can visualize himself as he performed his daily duties. The gavel represents an important part of Henry's routine as district magistrate and this artifact provides the springboard for many of his stories.

For Christine Newhard, her memories of her grandmother, the special cake, and the handed-down recipe are all personal artifacts that help her to relate her story to her third-grade students. They give a clearer understanding of her family background and how important her roots and traditions are to her. In addition, she reads aloud from *Knots on a Counting Rope* by Bill Martin Jr. and John Archambault. After discussing the importance of the boy's name and his relationship with his grandparents, the students are assigned to interview their grandparents to investigate foods and traditions of their culture. The culminating activity for this social studies unit was a "Food Fest" featuring many ethnic and traditional dishes. While sampling the foods, parents and grandparents shared their stories with all the students in the class.

All the aforementioned interviewees have artifacts that make the telling of their lives interesting, tangible, and memorable. It's not merely for the oral history process that artifacts wear a regal robe. Neuman and Bredekamp reported in Strickland and Morrow (2000) that some students start collecting and sharing artifacts early in their lives. Kindergarten teacher Tonya Beck has each of her students bring in a shoebox that transforms into a special treasure chest. Students place important items in the chest that will help them tell their stories. Some items the children have brought include their favorite Beanie Babies animals or photographs of places they have gone. The students are encouraged to add or take away items throughout the year. These items help to generate their ideas making story time interesting and enjoyable for the listeners (Strickland and Morrow 2000).

Another primary activity is called "A Multicultural 'Me Museum'" (Galda and Cullinan in Strickland and Morrow 2000). David Conway, a second-grade teacher, teaches an extensive thematic unit that introduces the circle of family, friends, and people in the child's life. His goal is to help his students see that people who care for them surround them. One activity in the unit is the "Me Museum": a section of the classroom is set aside where each student, one week at a time, displays items that depict their personality and background culture. Some of the items displayed were special books, photographs, cultural clothing, and other autobiographical items from their early life (for example, their baby shoes). During a designated time during the week, the child of the week "on display" tells about her selections and either reads

Figure 2–2 The book angel is an artifact that symbolizes the language arts career of a retired reading specialist.

aloud a book or poem or tells a family story. Conway feels this activity helps the students to appreciate each other and is "an extremely rewarding experience" for the child (Strickland and Morrow 2000).

Artifacts are often keepsakes that have symbolic representations of events attached. For Donna, a librarian aide, the scarf that she painted ten years ago is symbolic of the love she has for her teenage daughter Nicole. The personal inscriptions on the scarf will always be cherished by both of them, even as they are shared with others. The scarf helps Donna relate her stories of her love for the arts and music as well as the growing-up years of her daughter to anyone who asks her whenever she wears her scarf.

Sometimes keepsakes such as jewelry, pottery, and statues are symbolic artifacts (Figure 2–2). One piece of jewelry that often has a story attached is a ring, whether it is the diamond engagement ring, the wedding band, or another ring that holds special memories. For the late Steve Uivary, a retired community member, it was his ruby ring with a diamond that was awarded to him by American Bowling Congress for a perfect 300 game that he rolled during sanctioned league play. The ring was the artifact that reminded him of his bowling saga—over sixty years of stories that began with pin setting when he was not even a teenager to his last participation, representing his state at a retired citizens' bowling tournament in Orlando, Florida. Pottery that has been hand crafted and in the family for years may also have special significance

Figure 2–3 These bowls represent a memory of Diane's mother's love of cooking.

(Figure 2–3). There are a plethora of objects, events, and places that are often used as artifacts (see Appendix 2–A, Sample Artifacts).

When teaching your students about artifacts and their importance, instruction comes first. The students must know and understand what an artifact is. It is related to some important aspect of the interviewee's life. It can represent a hobby or event that recalls the past; it can represent a person who was a major influence to the interviewee. These artifacts are shared along with the interviewees' stories during the interview process (Figure 2–4).

To guide your students' understanding, give an example from your own life. Wear a piece of jewelry or talk about your wedding ring. Explain what it means to you and tell the story connected with it. Explain that it is an item that reminds you of the person who gave it to you, why you received it, and what event prompted the gift. Let the students hear and see how the artifact helps with your memories as you tell your story.

Model for your students by showing artifacts from your wallet. Your driving license is an artifact as are many of the photographs you have in your possession.

CD Connection

Go to the Gallery in the upper right-hand corner, and scroll down to the Artifacts Module, Teacher And Student Describe Artifacts Process.

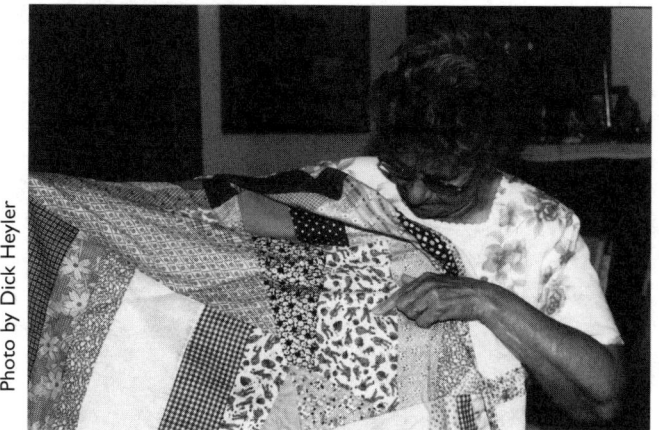

Figure 2–4 Dorna Heyler pointing to a patch of a dress she wore as a child. The quilt is made up of her mother's and sisters' dresses from 1900 to the 1930s.

Model by explaining an important person or event in your life. Perhaps you have a story to tell about 9/11/01 or a story about your parents or grandparents. Let the students practice with artifacts. They can bring an object in a brown paper bag and describe the object telling their stories. The listeners can try to figure out what is in the bag.

Model by explaining the significance of your name. Who named you? Why were you named your name? What is the significance of your family name? Do you like your name? Why or why not?

Students can then practice by finding out the significance of their names. They can ask relatives and bring their stories of their names to a sharing circle. Another way the students can practice is by thinking of an event that has happened that has influenced their lives. Newspapers and the Internet are good conduits for this activity. They could read what happened in history fifty years earlier than the present date.

Once students have learned the importance that artifacts play in a person's story, they are ready to interview others and interact with the person and his story through his artifacts. Open-ended statements such as, "Tell me more about this item (person, event)" or "Why is this item (person, event) important to you?" will encourage the person to tell the details of his story. Often these are at the initial point of the interview and help to get the interviewee thinking and talking about his past. One interviewee expressed her love of travel; therefore, the places she had gone and the people she met along the way were artifacts that led to further discussion. Many times elders

Figure 2–5 A shaving mirror belonging to grandfather Mudge used after the Civil War era.

will speak of important historical dates while relating their stories. All of these artifacts conjure the memories needed to add the details to their lives.

Artifacts come in all shapes and sizes and many different forms (Figure 2–5). Recognizing their importance gives the interviewer a greater depth of understanding of the person's story. Small treasures can remind people of significant people, events, and places in their lives. These keepsakes preserve the memories locked inside the storytellers' hearts. Through these treasures, the story becomes more vivid in his mind and easier to tell.

Books That Support Instruction on Artifacts

There are numerous picture books and young adult novels that can be shared to help students understand the importance of artifacts. These stories can be read aloud and discussed with your students.

Picture Books
Ruby's Wish by Shirin Yim Bridges

Aunt Flossie's Hats by Eleanor Fitzgerald, illustrated by James Ransome

Wilfred Gordon McDonald Partridge by Mem Fox

Knots on a Counting Rope by Bill Martin, Jr. and John Archambault

The Perfume of Memory by Michelle Nikly, illustrated by Jean Claverie

Jemma's Journey by Trevor Romain, illustrated by Pat Lopez

Me and Mr. Mah by Andrea Spalding, illustrated by Janet Wilson

Young Adult Novels

Hope Was Here by Joan Bauer

Sky Memories by Pat Brisson

A Letter to Mrs. Roosevelt by Carmine Coco DeYoung

Sun and Spoon by Kevin Henkes

CD Connection

Go to the Main Menu and choose the Artifacts Module. Click on Resource Materials at the top right for additional book titles.

Artifacts are interrelated to the other components of the Oral History Project: interview, memoir, photograph, and news article. During the interview, they are used to bring stories to life. They often jog the interviewee's memories to recall the past. Artifacts also may give a specific focus for the memoir and can easily be incorporated into the person's feature article. Many times the interviewees like to include some artifacts in their photographs because they complement their lives.

Artifacts on the Triptych

Students gather objects or images of the person to add to the final product because the artifacts are an important aspect of the person's life. The interviewees share artifacts such as photographs of when they marched in the Mummer's Parade or places they have served in the military such as North Korea. If the interviewee does not have personal artifacts easily accessible, the students often find pictures depicting the specific artifacts on the Internet or through other sources. An example of this was the F4U Corsair plane flown in World War II by Jake Anthony or the interviewee's senior class picture from his high school yearbook. The students added these photographs, documents, and other memorabilia to the triptych so that these artifacts are a visual presentation of information relevant to the person's life. Some students have used an artifact for the background or border of the triptych. Others have created the board to look like a church or barn. Planning and organizing all of the information about the person on the board is an exciting, problem-solving process for middle-grade students.

Assessment of Artifacts

Students may help create the rubric or checklist that will guide them with the artifacts on the triptych. Some questions that may be on a self-reflection checklist would include:

1. Are there a variety of artifacts representing the person's life?
2. Are the artifacts directly related to the person's life?
3. Are the artifacts interesting? Do they lead to questions about the person's life?
4. Are the artifacts organized in an eye-catching, appealing manner?
5. Are the artifacts related to the written pieces on the triptych?

When Lorraine Brong came from the senior citizen group that meets at her local church, she brought her paintings with her to share her hard work and accomplishments. She explained how the paintings have influenced her life. Henry McCool shared the gavel with the boys, telling them of the many interesting cases he had heard over the years. Christine Newhard shared photographs of her grandmother and the famous Dobos Torte as well as the tattered recipe in her grandmother's handwriting. Each individual had personal and relevant artifacts that were the impetus for rich stories. In the first two cases, the artifacts provided valuable information for the memoir and feature article that were composed for the Oral History Project. Artifacts are visual representations that complement both the memoir and the feature article that are the verbal representations of the person's life depicted on the triptych.

Appendix 2—A Sample Artifacts

The following list contains some items that have been used as artifacts to jog memories.

artwork	books	cards
charms	china	cookie cutters
cups	diaries	documents
family photographs	fishing equipment (lures)	gavels
golf balls	hockey sticks	jewelry
key chains	mirrors	music
necklaces	newspaper clippings	paintings
pianos	pottery	quilts
recipes	rings	road maps
scarves	seashells	shoes, sneakers
songs	statues	stopwatches
stuffed animals	tennis racquets	ticket stubs
war memorabilia	watches	
wedding photographs	yearbooks	

The following list reflects types of people who might be used as artifacts within the interviewee's story.

actors	astronauts	authors
celebrities	friends	sports figures
presidents	teachers	

relatives (parents, grandparents, siblings, aunts, uncles, cousins)

The following list offers some events that may be used to tell stories.

death of President Kennedy		death of Robert Kennedy
death of Martin Luther King		the Great Depression
Korean War	moon landing	space exploration
Vietnam War	Woodstock	World War II

Appendix 2–B Reflection Sheet

Chapter 2: Artifacts

What is my response to the opening thoughts and questions (*in italics*)?

What was the most valuable information that I gained personally and/or for my classroom?

What do I still need to know more about? Where could I go to get that information?

What ideas can I add to what I've already learned?

3 Research

Figure 3–1 Student compiles research for the Oral History Project.

Think about the last time that you wanted to find out some information about a person, place, or event. Where did you go to find that information? Who did you ask? Did the information create more questions that needed to be answered?

I first thought I could really interview PopPop without much research and still have a cool product. But when I was making up the questions to ask PopPop about what he did in World War II, I realized I really needed to know more so he could tell me about this unique experience. So, I figured I'd do a little more research such as to look at what a soldier's life was like. Then I remembered Dad telling me about PopPop being one of the many soldiers missing in action during the war after his ship was sunk; so I knew I wanted to know more about what that was like and what happened and how long he was called a missing person. Dad also told me the name of

47

the ship that PopPop'd been on was the SS *Leopoldville* and that he'd gotten a Purple Heart for what he did that evening long ago when it sank. I wanted to know what he did to earn the medal and if it was shaped like a Purple Heart and even if he'd show me his medal. I also wondered about what he'd done on that ship before it was hit and then sank. He never talked about the war before to any of us kids; yet I wanted to hear his stories. I remembered that Dad told me the *Leopoldville* was the only American ship sunk in the English Channel during the war. So, I looked up the ship on the Internet and in some book Dad had, by the same name. I found out so much about the *Leopoldville*, like it went down Christmas Eve. I learned later from PopPop that the survivors of that ship weren't even allowed to tell their families or anyone that they were even on the ship until 50 years after the war was over. So I had lots of questions about why that was. But I also wanted to know if it was snowing that Christmas Eve in 1944 over the channel; if the waters were choppy and cold; if it was pitch black, or if the sailors could see each other, or even if they could see land. I wanted to know how long they were in the water and how many of the soldiers like his friends even made it back with him. I didn't know if I could ask him about those who might have died all around PopPop. But I thought if I could get him to begin a story, I might find out and then later, he could capture that experience in a memoir that I needed to ask him to write anyway to include in my project. I also wanted to know if all those sailors who promised to be quiet about their experience actually did not say anything at all. I learned later, during the interview, that PopPop and his friend, Gilly, actually did keep their promise and that PopPop still didn't like to talk about that terrible night—even to me. The information I gathered about the ship on that night long ago helped me know what kind of questions I needed to ask to get him to tell me his story.

—K. M. Reilly

How do I find out about a topic? What places, people or things can I use to find out? For any learner, doing research can be exciting, uncovering and discovering information that leads to more questions, finding out more answers, and posing even more questions. In the anecdote above, the student already had a few ideas about her grandfather. Some of her ideas about her grandfather she actually experienced; but some of her ideas she learned from others, while growing up. Often, her ideas about her grandfather reflect such a blending of her experiences with others' experiences that she may find the lines blurred. Nevertheless, she wants to know more about each idea that she does have about him, so she can begin formulating questions to ask her grandfather about a particular time in his life. She can also think about ways to clarify her knowledge about events in his life. To help her in this endeavor, she begins to organize her search. For instance, if she divides her paper in half, she can write down what she already knows about him in one column and what she needs to know about him in the other column. This process helps her focus on the task of creating questions to find out enough information about her grandfather from his perspective. She ultimately will use this information that will include his stories and his artifacts to help her write a feature article about him (see Feature Article, Chapter 4). Further, all of the information she finds, learns, and writes about her grandfather will assist her later when she assembles a triptych or storyboard about him to share with others during her presentation about what she has learned (see Presentation, Chapter 7). However, before she can share in her presentation what she has learned and will learn about her grandfather, she needs to do some research.

Her teacher assists this student's enthusiasm and focus when she states and writes the objective of the task clearly on the board. The students see that the objective supports the daily selected activities that deal with research and all the other tasks in this Oral History Project. Further, it encourages all of the students throughout their narrowing search and documentation of their results of that search in ways that actively and meaningfully engage each student. The objective for doing research may be complex, but it is not complicated. It is multifaceted, but not difficult. Ultimately, every student learns that doing research for the Oral History Project will occur throughout the entire project, according to the specific needs of each student.

Research—An Ongoing Process, Rather Than an Event

Research for students, as any researcher learns, becomes an ongoing process that is tied to meaning (Poorman and Wright 2000). When students realize that initial research will assist them before they begin their interview, making the interview process easier and smoother for them, they generally do more than they are asked. Viewing research as an ongoing process has such a positive outcome for everyone who participates and internalizes this concept that it easily transfers to other situations when research is done in other classes (Grushka, Hinde-McLeod and Reynolds 2004). Because each student interviews a different person, the research each student does becomes a personal search for information that no one else can possibly lay claim to in the final product. It is, therefore, a personal and unique experiential process that engages each student, even as the process accompanies the student in other research settings much later. Another outcome features the students as creators of an original piece of research on a topic about which others may read and later refer. It is thrilling for students to realize that they are going to be involved in doing original research. They are hooked and excited.

Where Does it Begin? Laying the Groundwork

The initial research for the Oral History Project takes place as soon as the student selects the person to be interviewed. In K. M. Reilly's case, she selected her grandfather. Her teacher capitalized on Reilly's expertise with the Internet by involving her in an active search, such as occurs with the scavenger hunt. Similarly as with other students, the Internet represents one of the main technological methods that students use consistently to learn about their world. Using what they already know in technology gives them myriad ways to succeed and build on that success. When they succeed, they not only feel good about themselves and their abilities, they want to do more.

To build on that expertise as well as to model for Reilly and the other students in the class, a scavenger hunt activity using the overhead or computer technology to reflect images on the board can take place. Put three questions on the screen that will begin the students' search following the teacher's model.

1. What two events appeared in the newspaper on the date that my grandmother was born?
2. What two famous persons were born on the same date? (Follow-up question possibility: Why are they famous?)
3. What two important social, cultural, political, or economic events occurred on the date my grandmother was born? (Follow-up question possibilities: Describe ways that make them important still. Describe ways and possible reasons they are no longer important.)

Following the hunt and the discussion, ask the students to engage in their own personal scavenger hunt to find one answer for each of the three questions modeled above using their own interviewees' information. For example, one question that Reilly searched for on the Internet involved listing two events that occurred on the day that Reilly's grandfather was born. From these two choices, Reilly picked one, as indicated by the assignment. This and the other tasks gave her a sense of chronology and content, two important pieces of information providing greater meaning and context in understanding her grandfather's artifacts shared with her later during the interview.

A second search looked for famous people born on the same day as Reilly's grandfather. Because her grandfather was also a musician, a third search looked for other musicians who played during the time period to aide her interpretation of cultural, social, and economic issues. Because her grandfather lived in Philadelphia, Reilly narrowed her search to look specifically at musicians who played in Philadelphia during that era. Little by little, Reilly, as with each student in the class, found out more and more about such issues as the music, the cultural or social issues and events, the places, and the people who were a part of the time when her grandfather was born. While she gathered information, she found herself narrowing her search. She could not look up everything, nor could she put everything she found into the feature article about her grandfather.

All of this researched information forged an important perspective and became a part of the beginning piece when all parts of the puzzle later came together to create one particular aspect of K. M. Reilly's grandfather's story, before even interviewing him. This particular type of information gave her an idea of questions to ask during the interview process. It also helped her confidence level because she learned some peripheral information about the time, the places, the events, and some of the cultural features that existed during the time her grandfather was born.

This initial research functionally provided a solid jumping-off point from which to begin to shape her interview. On the Internet, she accessed magazine and newspaper articles to get more perspectives about the different eras in her grandfather's life. She got a more direct feeling for the historical and social time frame, so she eventually could frame questions that would be of his time and not before. Because she wanted to know about, record, honor, and frame his particular experience in his particular part of the world during his particular time of life, this research was crucial. The resulting interview material reflected *his* time, *his* experiences, and *his* take on different aspects of life. It provided a rich perspective that did not appear in most history books.

Other Valuable and Valid Places to Engage in Research

This type of research is only one way to begin the process of gathering information. Teachers know there are many other ways to show students that every community offers information in places that extend beyond computer use. The scavenger hunt activity uses the computer as but one tool of research, not as the sole tool for finding out information or different perspectives.

Another tool involves becoming competent in a library or a museum. For instance, one activity that engages students in the research process in a library or a museum is to find a piece of music composed on the day, the month, or the year the students were born. Ask the students to consider one of the following two questions: What is the name of a particular choice of music? Give a specific piece, not an entire genre. Perhaps several artists performed this piece. If so, and it is important to you, add the person or group's name. Describe the importance your music's subject, lyrics, or beat offers you in your life. Does hearing a specific song evoke a certain memory or feeling? If so, describe it.

CD Connection

Go to the Main Menu and click on the Gallery. Scroll down to Research Module, Librarian Introduces Different Methods of Research to Students.

Taking ten minutes, the students write down specific thoughts to answer *one* of the questions. When the students are finished, they share their findings with the class. Finally, they select one student's reflection that they have heard and write one or two sentences describing what the person shared with the class.

This activity is useful from a variety of levels. First, it helps students to see that there may be similar but also very different answers to the same question. The answers demonstrate perspective. Knowing there are many perspectives is vitally important for all students to recognize. The students also learn that the comments, while perceptions of a *specific* student, are based on a common knowledge of music they *all* share. Finally, they practice listening skills that later they will hone prior to conducting their interview.

Hence, students learn that information comes from a host of sources. Information found in a museum, a library, via the Internet, as well as from questions asked of an individual reflect valuable and diverse source choices. Similarly, students learn that accessing specific music, dances, or plays, as well as books and artifacts, also reflect valid and valuable ways to find out information and perspective. Finally, students grow to understand the importance of a person's recollections as another valuable source of information and perspective when conducting research on a topic.

Another Activity That Focuses on an Oral History Perspective

In another activity, ask the students to choose one question from a list. They are then to ask that question to a grandparent or a neighbor who is at least forty years older than the student. Some sample questions from the list follow.

1. When you were little, what games did you play? (Follow-up question possibilities: With whom did you play? Where did you play? What time of day?)
2. What did people in your family do for fun? (Follow-up question possibilities: What time of day? During which days—weekends? After school? After work? After dinner? Never on Sundays? Describe a specific memory at a specific time.)

CD Connection

Go to Main Menu and click on Gallery. Scroll down to Research Module, Thoughts on the Value of Knowing How to Research.

Whatever the activity, the important piece is to get students to see there are many ways to find out information. Using only one mode often limits the way to view the world. The scavenger hunt, the library or museum search, asking a grandparent or elder neighbor a question all launch students into discovery using research to answer their questions.

Through modeling, discussing, and implementing many ways to do research, the students learn that each method has value, particularly when it answers a question that is important for the researcher to know. As a result, students understand the relevance and the crucial importance of finding out more information about an idea, an artifact, an important date, and so forth that leads to interacting with research through a *variety* of modes. Further, as you demonstrate the concepts, skills, products, and assessment criteria, the students will be prepared for the experience. Their initial research creates a knowledge base showing them the distinct advantage they have as interviewers prior to and during the actual interview that occurs later. With initial research, the interviewer learns to work smarter, not harder.

As previously stated, research reflects an ongoing process, rather than merely an event experienced once or twice. In the interview chapter, the research process is done as the students learn more about their interviewees. To support the students' understanding that research is recursive, an overview of each part of the research component is posted (see Figure 3–2, page 56). This will assist the students to visualize where they will be going, what they will be doing and when they will be doing it, as they understand ways the concepts, skills, products, and assessment criteria interrelate in this project. Research incorporates the following:

Concepts
1. Understanding there is credible and dependable information from a host of sources including materials found in libraries and museums, from people, and via the Internet.
2. Understanding there is appropriate and relevant information to identify and acquire for any subject chosen.
3. Understanding that collaboration can help the student clarify and learn more about the subject.

Skills
1. Discerns what is credible, dependable, and relevant information.
    a. in books
    b. on the Internet
    c. in primary and secondary sources
2. Learns that information comes from various sources.
    a. museums
    b. people
    c. Internet
    d. books
    e. libraries
    f. historical sites and documents, and/or artifacts
3. Works collaboratively to understand, learn, clarify, and process information.
4. Uses correct documentation, which includes primary and secondary resources, according to the level of student learning.

Products
1. Notes and/or log of research activities
    a. On note cards (see Sample Note Card formats in the Appendix, 3–A)
        1. Each card has a topic at the top, the source, the date the information was retrieved, and a brief paragraph of the contents found from that information.
        2. The cards effectively organize the search for information about the interviewee to assist the student in the interview, the feature article, and the memoir.
    b. In a notebook
        1. An entry appears in paragraph form on separate pages, dated and cited for easy retrieval and documentation.
        2. It organizes the search for information about the interviewee to assist the student in the feature article and memoir.
        3. Key points show what the student did during the research process, including successes and setbacks.
2. Information and/or images related to the subject researched
    a. Documents
    b. Artifacts such as photos, medals, and/or citations, objects (refer to the Artifacts chapter)
3. Possible list of primary and secondary resources
    a. Using documents either shared by the person interviewed or found out about the subject prior to the interview, the student-interviewer generates more questions to pose.
    b. Primary and secondary resources validate the research process engaged in by both the interviewer and the interviewee.
4. Questions generated from research for the interview
    a. Open-ended questions, designed to obtain more information on a subject rather than elicit only a "yes" or "no" response from the interviewee.
    b. Close-ended questions, designed to elicit a "yes" or "no" response.

Assessment criteria (see Sample Assessment Checklist in the Appendix, 3–B)
1. Information is properly documented and is relevant to the subject.
2. Sources demonstrate authenticity and diversity, such as community members, museum, library, historical sites, Historical Society, and Internet use.

3. Rubrics
    a. Selected or formulated by the teacher
    b. Selected or formulated by the students with guidance from the teacher

Students will do the following:

Access information	Choose relevant information	Select documented information pertinent to the subject
Locate information using appropriate strategies and sources: • Library • People • Museums • Historical Society • Internet • Historical sites	• Relate directly to person, place, or event • Cross-check references with other sources	Organize and present selected ideas from research

Figure 3–2 Concepts, skills, products and assessment and their relationship to research.

More Activities!

Other teaching activities that engage a group of students in the research process are as follows:

1. In "hide and seek," each group or individual student selects one of several written, focused subjects or questions on 3 x 5-inch cards. The designated subject or question on the card, researched and answered within a brief time, is shared with everyone in a single class period. In addition, there is student reflection time that addresses the students' focus on the value of the three methods used to find the answer.

    For example, Fred picks a card:

    "Who was one of the early eighteenth-century architects of the Huntingdon Borough's first fifty-two houses?" Because Fred has talked about and practiced using diverse choices for doing research, he knows he has many sources to help him find the answer. He can choose to use the Internet; the library; the Historical Society, where he either asks the curator or looks at the resources; or he can ask his social studies teacher who knows about Pennsylvania history, especially her community's history.

George, who sits next to Fred, feels very lucky because he loves old rock and roll. His question asks: "Where is Jim Morrison of the Doors buried?" He already knows the answer to the question because he is such a fan. Still, he knows he needs to put down his source, so he goes to the Internet, and becomes surprised at what he finds. He always thought Morrison was buried in Paris, but now he finds out Jim's family moved his body, although the headstone is still in the Père Lachaise Cemetery. He tells some of his music buddies and they are in disbelief. He goes to another source only to find his previously held belief was incorrect. He quietly notes it on his card, in awe.

2. In another activity, "birth date," either individually or in small groups, students find out what happened on the day they were born. After a specific birth date, such as Abraham Lincoln's, is briefly modeled, the students' hunt is on! The students become elated, engaged, and hooked into finding out what occurred on *their* date of birth. The room is vibrant with the chatter as the students share their discoveries.

In both of these interactive teaching activities, students are engaging in positive opportunities for problem solving and using a variety of research methods to obtain their answers. Once students are comfortable with these guided research activities, they may move to a subject that the entire class of students will work on cooperatively. For example, the students involve their families by asking them about a business or building that existed in the community when they were young. Perhaps it houses a different business now than a generation ago. Perhaps the building has been restructured or the business has been modified.

The students bring in the names of their places to be compiled in a class list, with the most often mentioned spot to become the subject of class research. From this point, each student becomes responsible for a part of the research process. For instance, one student searches when the original structure was built. Another student researches which company and architect built it. Another looks at any transformations of its structure that took place over a twenty-year period, as with an addition of a porch, window treatments, retrofitting a coal firebox to oil, and so forth. Another student looks for historical events that occurred during some of the changes. Still another uncovers the various uses of the structure from one time period to another. The possibilities for this type of activity are quite endless and pertinent to the students' lives.

For this activity, the emphasis is on both the process and the product and is accomplished within a relatively short period of time. Having a product within a short period of time serves many purposes. It underlines the need to establish a narrow, tight focus for exploration. It demonstrates the importance of tending to research matters promptly to meet deadlines. Finally, it stresses the importance of collaboration in a problem-solving manner to find information.

Conferencing

Providing class time for the students and the teacher to conference is very productive and essential. Following or during the conference period, the students might complete a checklist, make anecdotal notes, or write a one-page summary of the conference in their notebooks to practice an important aspect of listening skills as well as to get them to take and make notes. Initially, the teacher models this difficult and important skill for the students to become familiar with, telling them it can evolve with them as they grow from primary- to secondary-grade levels. Consider the following scenario:

Teacher: Hi, Sophie. Tell me what you found so far with your research on the process of making paper pads at the Blair Building.

Student: It's really cool, Ms. R. I learned that the glue they used was stored in a very large container—a vat. They at first used large pieces of wet canvas to cover the containers to keep the glue from drying out.

Teacher: That's fascinating, Sophie. Was this information difficult to find? Which sources did you use to find out that information?

Student: I guess I had a small question 'cause I read about it in some materials at the Historical Society. I also asked Ms. S, who is the curator there. She told me more about it and also some other cool things. I can't wait to go back to go through some more stuff that she has.

After their discussion that includes difficulties encountered and ways the student problem solved to turn them into successes, the student and teacher write a brief paragraph about what they covered during their conference and what Sophie's next goals will be. They share their paragraphs and end the conference (see sample Conference Form in the Appendix, 3–D).

Many districts have documentation preferences listed in their curricula, which students follow as early as possible to get them familiar with the format and documentation process. When the process is modeled and practiced, students learn simple speaking and listening skills accompanied with documenting research in various ways. As the skills are practiced in large- and small-group settings, students become comfortable using them.

It is crucial to get students to use research as an ongoing, recursive process, rather than one composed of isolated events. It is motivational for students to learn to ask questions and seek answers about topics in which they are genuinely interested. Guide students to reach that level of understanding as they seek and find answers to many questions. If they practice using a variety of sources, students learn there are many perspectives involved when answering questions. They discover that rich and often complex perspectives enhance facts. Throughout many of the components of this Oral History Project, research is an interwoven framework.

For more information on the research process:

Hoopes, James. 1979. *Oral History: An Introduction for Students*. Chapel Hill, NC: University of North Carolina Press. Library of Congress. www.loc.gov/americaslibrary.

Poorman, Linda and Mary Wright. 2000. "Middle School Students Learning to Research: An Inquiry-Based Approach." In Maureen McLaughlin and Mary Ellen Vogt (editors), *Creativity and Innovation in Content Area Teaching*. Norwood, MA: Christpoher-Gorden Publishers, Inc.

Appendix 3—A Sample Note Card Format:

Name:	Date:
Topic:	Source:
Notes:	

Appendix 3–B Sample Assessment Checklist for Documentation

Book:

I have the following details:

1. author's last name, first name, initial
2. year of publication in parenthesis
3. italicized title
4. place where published
5. publisher

Example: King, M. L., Jr. (1998). *The Autobiography of Martin Luther King, Jr.* New York: Warner Books, Inc.

Appendix 3–C Sample Note-taking Sheet #1

Name: _____ Topic: _____ Date: _____

My question: _____

Notes   Source

Sample Note-taking Sheet #2

Name: _____ Topic: _____

Key words   Notes   Source

Comments

Appendix 3–D Conference Form

Name: _____ Date: _____

Subject: _____

Summary:

You may want to include some of the following questions:

> What are you enjoying the most so far?
> What are some of the difficulties you're experiencing at this stage of the task? What steps are you using to deal with those difficulties?
> What ways have you communicated your successes?
> What's been the most fun? What did you learn?

1.

2.

3.

4.

5.

Other comments:

Student's initials: _____   Teacher's initials: _____

Appendix 3–E Reflection Sheet

Chapter 3: Research

What is my response to the opening thoughts and questions (*in italics*)?

What was the most valuable information that I gained personally and/or for my classroom?

What do I still need to know more about? Where could I go to get that information?

What ideas can I add to what I've already learned?

4 Feature Article

Figure 4–1 Historical newspapers are an invaluable resource as students write their feature articles.

Think of a feature article you read that made an impact on you. What made this article different from a typical news article, and what was the impact it made on you?

Lindsay, a red-haired eighth grader, discovered that one trip to her grandmother's house was not enough to complete her interview for the Oral History Project. In fact, she found that when she returned to school after the first interview and started her research, she needed to go back to her grandmother to get clarification on some of the statements. Each time she went, her grandmother would bring out another artifact and tell another story. With each visit, Lindsay's notebook became more dog-eared as she entered more information to the pages. Finally, with a storehouse of notes, stories, and memories, Lindsay began her story. Before long, she had finished drafting her article and had gone, rough draft in hand, to visit her grandmother one more time.

"Mr. Smith, I showed my Gramma the feature article I did on her last night. She wanted to see that it was all right before I put it with the rest of my Oral History Project. When my Gramma read it, she said she was so proud of me."

"Well, you've done a great deal of work, Lindsay. You took many notes and had much information about your grandmother for your article. After all, not many women are still alive around here who actually witnessed a public hanging."

"Oh, Mr. Smith, it wasn't that."

"Well, must be you got all of the information about her life correct and presented it in order."

"She was happy about that, and getting in as much information as possible, but she said that it was the first time she had been written about in an actual newspaper."

"Lindsay, does she know that the article doesn't go in an actual newspaper, that it is an important part of your project?"

"Sure, she knows that it is for my project, but she felt that my article was good enough to be in an actual newspaper. She loved it and was proud of it. And, Mr. Smith, I am too."

The importance of the feature article cannot be stressed enough. This is the component of the Oral History Project that conveys not only the *who, what, when, where, why,* and *how* information about the subject, but it pulls together material from the interview, artifacts, and research. This information, once assembled, is then formed into the feature article, ready to be presented to the reader.

CD Connection

Go to Main Menu and click on Gallery. Scroll down to News Article Module; Video - Thoughts on the Value of the News Article.

The feature article is distinguishable from the normal news article in an important way. Although the type of writing is expository/informational, it is not the normal news story employed by most newspapers. A typical news story concentrates in a tight, informative lead, the first paragraph of the story packed with essential information; the structure employed in a news story is the inverted pyramid: the important information comes first and is followed by explanation of that information. If necessary, the editor may decide to begin at the end of the story and eliminate information in order to make the story "fit" the page. In this manner, a writer's story may be cut and information about the subject removed. The feature story, although similar in content to the news story, exists as a complete piece, to be revised but not to be cut from the end toward the beginning. The feature article allows a student to assemble information about the subject and exercise his writing skills.

Expository writing at the middle/junior high level can be dry and unexciting for many students; too often the writing is listlike, just a presentation of interview questions and answers. However, with the proper instruction, modeling, and guidance, the result can be writing that sparkles with information and style—it can be the type of writing that engages both the writer and the reader.

In feature writing, as opposed to journalistic writing, the emotional level is raised. Whereas journalistic writing goes for facts, feature writing allows for the human element, and that is what puts many students in closer contact with their subjects. This component allows the student to explore not only the history of the subject but also the emotions connected with that history. It combines subjectivity with objectivity.

The students are already familiar with the components of the project. When introducing the feature article, describe what a feature article is as well as the way the pieces fit together. Students need to know that the feature article uses the questions *who, what, when, where, why,* and *how* to generate the material for the story. The students

Figure 4–2 Janna Heyler talks with her grandmother about Janna's great-grandfather's shaving mirror.

will be using the information to craft a *lead, body,* and *conclusion* that does more than give a chronological story of the subject, but it will "feature" the subject in a way that positions her in terms of self, family, community, and history. The feature article is more than a simple list of happenings in the subject's life; it is a coherent piece of writing that reveals the person through information garnered from interview, artifacts, and research.

To fully craft a quality feature article, a student must first have completed a portion of the interview. Once the interview is at least partially complete, the student needs to have engaged in initial research and to have accessed one or more artifacts. By having the interview, research, and artifact component partially finished or complete, it is essential the student understand that the process is fluid and not chronological and know that he can return to the subject for more information, to research activities, and access more artifacts at any time during the process. Upon drafting a piece, the student must be able to add more information or search for more information to more fully create the final piece.

Once the students have enough information to begin, the teacher models the feature story in the following ways.

One way to model the feature story is to examine stories by professional writers. The Sunday edition of any newspaper is the best resource for feature stories about people, although feature stories about towns, animals, happenings, and phenomena also work. Find two to three quality articles and copy them for the entire class. Read the article aloud, discussing various elements of the feature story but not going into exhaustive detail on each point. The purpose of this whole-group activity is to introduce the concept by identifying it.

CD Connection

Go to Main Menu and click on Gallery. Scroll down to News Article Module; Video - Teacher Has Class Analyze Real News Articles As Example.

To provide an additional model after the articles are read and discussed, students are assigned to read newspapers in order to find a feature article of their own. Students then bring the articles to class and identify the elements of feature writing using their articles.

Student models, such as the one at the end of this chapter, also work well. This article about George Robertson's life resonates well with students. The article also successfully utilizes all the elements of feature article writing.

Access the feature articles included on the CD-ROM. These articles not only use the elements of feature writing, but they are written by teachers across all grade levels. The subject matter is highly engaging for students as they present people who learn, travel, have families, love, laugh, and succeed.

Once the class has examined models of well-written feature stories, it is time to practice writing feature articles. The following method, assembling and unscrambling a feature story, serves as a first practice session.

Assembling and Unscrambling a Feature Story

1. Scan newspapers and magazines for feature articles on people. Try to choose stories that encompass the feature article elements: lead, body, conclusion; who, what, when, where, why, and how. Again, the Sunday newspapers and Sunday newsmagazines usually have articles that work well.

2. Choose three or four articles; the goal is to choose articles with a mix of personalities that a boy or girl of middle school age would find interesting. Sports figures, national "heroes," "ordinary" people, and entertainment figures tend to be popular with students.

3. Next, retype the article in larger print.

4. Cut the sentences apart and separate them into categories that label the elements—that is, sentences from the lead go into an envelope marked "Lead," and so on.

5. In small groups, students choose an article and are given the envelopes. They are instructed to recreate or create a lead, body, and conclusion about their subject.

6. Once students have compiled their jigsaw feature articles, one member from each group reads the article out loud, so the others can hear different feature articles.

7. Finally students see the original article to let them see how their articles compare. Many times the students have compiled a feature article that rivals the craft of the original.

Once students have practiced this form of assembling a feature article, they are ready to prewrite for their own article. Armed with the knowledge of the feature article elements and their notes, students begin to identify information from the interviews they wish to include in the feature article. It is easy for students to slip into a formula writing style that will merely list information about the subject—circumstances of birth, growing up, and favorite things. A working outline of information will help them not only structure their articles but also sort through their notes to determine what is necessary at this writing.

In the working outlines strive to include the following information:
Lead
Body
   Biographical information
   Family information
   Qualities—What qualities does this person have that makes him or her stand apart from others?
   Impact—What impact, if any, has this person had on others?
   Events—What events has this person experienced in life? Has this person been part of any well-known "events" in history?
   Future—What plans does this person have for the future? What future does this person see for him or herself?
Conclusion

When beginning the project, some students used tape recorders to tape the interview, some students used notebooks to first write out questions leaving space to jot notes and quotes from the subject, and some students used loose-leaf papers that more times than not became hopelessly jumbled. After a couple years of this variety it was decided that the notebook approach was best to keep students at this age organized. This allowed those who want to tape the interview to do so; it also encourages students to keep a notebook of answers that will help them assemble the written pieces for the project.

Once the interview has been completed and the student has assembled the outline for the feature article, it is time to break out an invention that is readily used by even the most cynical student—the highlighter. Relatively inexpensive, it is wise to keep about thirty highlighters in the desk at all times. The florescent blue, yellow, pink, green, and orange colors are ready to be put to use.

On the inside of the notebook, have students write down their outline and then choose a different color for each major area. For example:

Section of the Article	Highlighted Color
lead	pink
biographical information	yellow
family information	green
qualities	blue
impact	orange
conclusion	pink and blue

As most highlighters come in five basic colors, students and teachers might need to consider combinations if the working outline has more than five components. Some areas may need to share colors. Once the information gleaned has been outlined, students can go through their interview material and notes, highlighting the respective areas. Students love this part of the process. They delight in highlighting their material to fit into their organizational plans. This guides students through their material and it helps them visually organize their information. When finished, not only do they have colorful interview material, they have organized their material and are now ready to write (Figure 3–4).

Figure 3–4 An eighth grade student uses highlighters to organize his feature article.

What you will encounter by using this visual process of organizing is that at-risk students are able to organize their interview notes at a rate that helps them draft a more comprehensive feature article. Many at-risk students have produced longer, more thoughtful feature articles using this method. Their feature articles tend to be crisper, deeper, more organized, and the whole process of creating a draft from notes is less stressful. The students who use this method are proud of their finished drafts and are ready to have them published with the stronger writers in their class.

After completing the working outline and identifying information from the interview, students begin writing their first drafts. They should be encouraged to follow their outlines, but they should realize it is acceptable to be flexible when it comes to omitting or including new information. During this draft writing, students begin to identify areas where they need to clarify something, or areas they neglected to ask about during the interview. Now is the time for them to contact their oral history subject again to clarify or gain additional material. Once students have finished their first draft, they revise it. Revision is done through peer conferencing, teacher conferencing, and self-revision techniques.

Concurrent with the instruction of the feature article, assessment of the feature article is explained to the students. The Pennsylvania State Writing Domain Rubric (see Appendix 4–A) encompasses the five characteristics/domains that ensure effective writing: focus, content, organization, style, and conventions. Each domain is addressed as students examine and compose their introduction/lead, body, and conclusion. There are other rubrics as well (see Appendix 4–B and 4–C for more sample rubrics for the feature article).

As the students are drafting their feature articles, they are making connections in several areas. Past practice has shown that students make connections from their own writing to writing found in newspapers and magazines. The information they have experienced in the past in informative writing now takes on a new meaning. Previously, students have used informative writing to explain directions, give reports, and investigate typical situations that require expository writing skills. This project gives the student a chance to simultaneously become a news reporter and feature reporter. Because many students are familiar with the subject from spending much of their childhood with them, they often think they know all about them. However, through this project, they tend to discover new information about the subject. This information, coupled with their immediate knowledge, usually creates a closer relationship that cannot be underestimated. Not only is a personal connection made with the subject, it is enhanced. The academic and personal connection to new situations is an important part of this transforming process. Students can read newspapers and comment on the lead of a local or national writer; this critical thinking helps them become middle school "experts" on published writing styles.

When the drafts have been revised and edited, new information added or old information clarified, students are ready to create their final copies, which will eventually be posted on the triptych. Quality is never a question when finishing these copies, for students now are excited to publish it on their triptychs. Their subjects are close to them, and the students are so involved they *want* to do the absolute best they can. They are writing for more than the project; they are writing an authentic piece featuring the life of a person they have come to know more intimately. They are now transferring their knowledge of writing and gathering personal history into a finished product that highlights someone they care about.

The feature article accomplishes several goals. First of all, this type of writing can be flat and uninteresting if not done carefully; it is a style of writing students will be doing often in the future, in high school, college, or the workplace. The goal is to use an authentic situation to enhance this writing style. Another goal is to explain important information for the oral history project itself—after all, this is the written information about the subject that explains the artifacts and identifies qualities and ideas about the subject that might otherwise not be included on the triptych display. In most standards-based schools, informative writing is found in nearly every benchmark. But most importantly, at the middle school level, a goal is to use a real-life experience to teach writing, organization, and respect.

The feature article has three parts to its structure: the *lead, body,* and *conclusion*. It is the interview that supplies the *who, what, when, where, why,* and *how* content material, but it is the structure that efficiently puts forth this information.

Before beginning to build the article, with interview notes and tapes in hand, students first review the information and then, using prewriting strategies, they sketch out the basic details of the article (Figure 4–4). Once the prewriting is finished, have a guide on a page or two that

CD Connection

Go to Main Menu and click on Gallery. Scroll down to News Article Module; Video - Teacher Explains The 5 W's And The Lead Paragraph.

Figure 4–4 This student used prewriting strategies by sketching out details for his article from his notes.

visually allows the student to organize and then direct information from the interview.

Lead: The Beginning of the Feature Article

The lead for a feature article is different from a typical news lead in that it does not always try to get out the important who, what, when, where, why, and how information in the first couple of paragraphs. The "hard" lead is used in most news stories, but the lead employed in feature article writing is a "soft" lead, crafted by students once they have their information.

Students can craft this lead at different points in the process. Some students like to write the lead first and let it guide them through creating the body. Other students like to write the body first and then write the lead once they have internalized the article and information. Successful leads are written in both ways, so let the students be responsible for this choice. If a student is having difficulty in getting started on any part of the article, suggest a "working" lead, one that may be retooled later for the lead used or one that may be disregarded when the body is finished and the student has a new direction with new ideas for the lead. However, stress that the lead needs to accomplish several tasks: The lead should somehow introduce the subject. "Somehow," because to avoid formulaic writing, and to craft stylistic writing the name of the person doesn't have to appear. There are ways to write leads without one hundred percent identification of the subject. Middle school students, when encouraged—and sometimes without any encouragement—try to experiment. This middle school rebellion—rather a harsh word for what it is—can be channeled into interesting writing.

The lead should set the tone of the piece. A dark somber lead should not introduce a comic piece; when students practice creating leads, they learn what tone is and ways to use it effectively.

The lead should be interesting. This is a must, even if it means many rewrites. A lead needs to engage the reader, and pull the reader into the piece. Just because the subject is the writer's grandmother does not mean that all people will take the time to read the whole piece, which is the goal of the writing—to have an audience read the whole piece as well as to explain the life of the subject.

A good lead needs to do more than inform the reader; it needs to evoke a personal response and an emotional response from the reader. These leads are about people who are in the lives of our students and so the emotional aspect becomes important. A lead to this type of article is usually longer than one to a regular news story.

There are different ways to create a lead. As all students are different, the lead form they choose will lend strength to their feature article.

Types of Leads

An Anecdote   Basically, an anecdote is a brief story that reflects the subject and the larger article. The anecdote sets the tone of the piece and also sets the tone of the subject. Anecdotes draw the reader into the life of the subject as well as the article. All good anecdotes contain some forms of conflict and drama, whether that conflict and drama are humorous, tragic, sad, or aggressive.

Following is an example of an anecdote.

> Thirty-five years ago, in March, our whole family was struggling with a spring snow that had blanketed the area. This ten inches of snow happened at a bad time as we were in tapping the maple trees in the sugar bush, getting ready for syrup making. With about one quarter of the trees tapped, we had several hundred to attend to, and we had to walk through the forest doing this. There

was only one tractor but several roads. I was sent to tap the trees on the upper road, and being 12 years old, I was proud to be out on my own, frustrated to have to trudge through an additional 10 inches of snow, and a bit scared as the sun was starting to go low in the sky and the tree shadows got longer and longer. I knew I'd be at least a quarter mile from the rest of the men tapping, and I was the youngest.

After an hour of walking up the road, my hands were cold from pounding the metal taps into the maple trees. My feet were cold and my legs ached. About that time, I heard a rustling noise behind me; I turned and could see no one. I went back to tapping. A few minutes later I heard the noise again. I thought of the rumors about wildcats and bears. I started getting scared.

Two more taps in the trees. There were 10 more left in my pouch. I heard the rustle of branches again. The shadows moved as the noise drew closer. One more tap in. Another one. The rustling sound was closer; then I heard a branch crack. I dropped a tap into the snow and reached through the tap-shaped hole in the snow to retrieve it.

Another tap in. Snap! I turned, and there, running across the road not twenty feet in front of me was a bobcat, gray and brown, running through the snow, past the trees I had tapped. As it ran off through the forest, I gathered my bag of taps and hammer and realized that I had no more taps: I had finished the job! Controlling my shaking arms and legs, I returned to the syrup shed having finished my job.

This anecdote highlights the fear of the subject when he was twelve years old. It shows a strength that the writer will develop into a theme of strength of the farm boy who goes off to war, returns successfully, and embarks on raising a family and pursuing a career in farming.

A Quotation
The use of a quotation or brief monologue by the subject often serves to highlight a theme in the article. It also serves to engage the reader by allowing the subject to speak directly to the audience, as in the following example:

> "What did you do to that dog?" His voice raised not in anger, but in incredulity. "Why on earth did you shave off all his hair? I know you're upset, but to shave the dog?" The father looked down at both his son and the panting, tail wagging dog standing in a pile of gray and black hair.

> "I hope someday you learn to channel your energies into good things, and never work at the SPCA." Suppressing a laugh, he turned and walked away from his son, the dog, and the pile of hair.

In that creative and non-aggressive reaction to his son's actions, the subject defined himself as a man who found humor in a situation instead of choosing it as an avenue toward punishment.

The best quotations are not lengthy and didactic; they tend to be shorter and reveal something about the subject. They can be used to elicit a laugh, to shock, to inform, or to describe. A quotation should illustrate something about the subject that will later be explained in the article.

Description

> She has salt-and-pepper gray hair, pulled back tightly and wound in a braided bun on the back of her head. She stands at a flour-covered counter in an otherwise spotless kitchen. Her wrinkled fingers are covered and she rolls and pushes down a softball-sized piece of bread dough. There is a white flour streak across her forehead, and her wire-rimmed glasses are perched halfway down her nose. Beside her right arm are four gray aluminum bread pans with more softball-sized loaves of dough, slowly beginning to rise in the pans.
>
> For years, this has been Lettie Andrews' Saturday routine. Up early in the morning, make breakfast, clear and wash the dishes, and then spend the rest of the day making 10 loaves of bread to last her small family for the week, saving two loaves for her neighbor across the road.

This description provides the reader not only with a physical description of this woman, but also a bit of her kitchen and her routine, which is in place to aid her family and her neighbors. From this lead, the reader can use words to picture this woman and to give voice to traits about her, traits that will be explained in the ensuing body of the feature article.

Although there are other types of leads—posing a question, using a quotation that highlights an aspect of the subject, summarizing a characteristic of the subject—I find that these three affect middle school students' success in beginning a feature article. They also call on other skills—narrative writing, word choice, showing and not telling, and creating interest. In the lead students can play with ways to introduce their oral history subject.

Body: The Heart of the Feature Article

The body of the feature article explains the subject, giving biographical information as well as descriptions of the qualities of that person. What qualities does the subject possess that sets her apart from others? Are these qualities personal and/or professional? In what ways have these qualities shaped this person's life?

Most middle school students will want to have some type of physical description of their subject in the body. Encourage them to use their subject's words via direct quotations as often as possible. By including description and direct words, the subject has a chance of appearing more vividly in the writing, which, after all, is the goal of this writing—to make it more vivid, interesting, and exact; to make it come alive for the reader. It is also important to encourage inclusion of anecdotes within the article, especially if the lead is not in the anecdotal structure. After all, narrative writing can be intertwined in expository writing to make it more exact. Plus, many of life's experiences are stories, waiting to be recorded as such.

As mentioned before, a danger in the body is that many students like to include as many of their subject's "favorites" as possible. By including many "favorites" the writing becomes a list of what the subject likes and even what the subject dislikes. However, by including anecdotes, experiences, descriptions, qualities, and quotations, the presentation is more likely to become a fully realized piece of writing rather than a laundry list.

To create the body, first help students understand types of order—chronological, importance, spatial, and logical—as well as transitional words and phrases. Organization is highly important in arranging information that could otherwise appear daunting to students.

Conclusion: Tying Together and Coming Full Circle

A successful conclusion will enhance a successful body and lead. A lead and conclusion form a partnership that serves not as decoration for the body and the information but to establish and then affirm the tone of the piece and the engagement of the reader. When the body is complete, it is then time to write the conclusion. By leaving off the conclusion the audience is left abruptly at the end of an otherwise engaging article. Students need to know that they have finished a piece of writing and have finished a complete thought process. The conclusion, unlike the lead, is written when the body is finished and it gives a sense of completeness to the writing. Although a lead brings the reader in, the conclusion allows the reader to reflect on the subject and the subject's life. As there are varieties to the lead, there are varieties to the conclusion, including, but not limited to the following.

Future Action
This conclusion may use the subject's words or a prediction by the writer to predict what the subject will do in the future. This step alludes to what the next step will be for the subject. It uses ideas and information presented, and sometimes actual words, to project the subject into the future.

Quotation
By using the subject's own words, the writer can end the piece with a glimpse into the personality of the subject. The tone of the whole essay can be echoed with a well-chosen quote from the interview.

Framework/Full-Circle Ending
The writer returns to ideas or experiences from the lead. By picking up elements from the lead—and not merely repeating them—the writer can create a framework that brings the audience and the subject back to ideas from the beginning, thus creating a feeling of completeness.

Description
Similar to using description for the beginning to establish ideas and personality, the writer can use a different description for the same reason in the end; now the ideas and personality have been established, they can be reaffirmed in the conclusion.

Summary
A favorite with students, they write a summary of the person as a way to explain what the life of the subject has been. Although feature writing is primarily exposition, at this point, many students will include commentary about how successful the subject has been in his life.

Revision

At this point, the draft is finished and it is time for revision. The following list of questions should be used for self- and peer revisions.

Does the article exhibit a consistent theme?

Does the article contain a consistent tone?

Is the writing free of clichés?

Does the writing contain strong verbs and specific words?

Is the writing logically organized?

Are transitional words and phrases used?

Are the quotations meaningful?

Does the lead set the tone, capture the reader's interest, and hint about or identify the subject?

Does the lead connect with the rest of the article?

Does the conclusion complete the story?

Once students have finished discussing and reflecting upon the revisions, it is time to include pertinent revisions into their work and bring it to final copy form. The writer creates a title, and then creates a final copy that is edited for correctness: mechanics, spelling, usage, punctuation, and capitalization. The finished product is a feature article that is affixed to and published on the triptych. (See Appendix 4–D for "The Life of George Robertson: A Mother's Worst Fear" by Nathan Close, whose prewriting is shown in Figure 4–4).

By following this format, the final copies have created, as Lindsay's grandmother noted, proud students and proud subjects. It is apparent that the writing is original and engaging. The authenticity of the project has a lasting effect on the students and their future writing. They become "feature article" experts, writing more descriptively, giving more quality, and exerting more effort. The feature article is a huge part of this transformational process; it connects students to their community and to another, larger community that extends far beyond their school and their families.

For more information on the feature article process:

Blundell, William E. 1988. *The Art and Craft of Feature Writing: Based on the Wall Street Journal Guide.* New York: Penguin.
Jackson, Dennis, and John Sweeny. 2002. *The Journalist's Craft: A Guide to Writing Better Stories.* New York: Allworth Press.
Sova, Dawn B. 1998. *How to Write Articles for Newspapers and Magazines.* Lawrenceville, NJ: Peterson's.

Appendix 4–A   Pennsylvania Writing Assessment Domain Scoring Guide

	Focus	Content	Organization	Style	Conventions
4	The single controlling point made with an awareness of task (mode) about a specific topic	The presence of ideas developed through facts, examples, anecdotes, details, opinions, statistics, reasons, and/or explanations.	The order developed and sustained within and across paragraphs using transitional devices including introduction and conclusion	The choice use and arrangement of words and sentence structures that create tone and voice	The use of grammar, mechanics, spelling, usage, and sentence formation
4	Sharp, distinct controlling point made about a single topic with evident awareness of task (mode)	Substantial, specific, and/or illustrative content demonstrating strong development and sophisticated ideas	Sophisticated arrangement of content with evident and/or subtle transitions	Precise, illustrative use of a variety of words and sentence structures to create consistent writer's voice and tone appropriate to audience	Evident control of grammar, mechanics, spelling, usage, and sentence formation
3	Apparent point made about a single topic with sufficient awareness of task (mode)	Sufficiently developed content with adequate elaboration or explanation	Functional arrangement of content that sustains a logical order with some evidence of transitions	Generic use of a variety of words and sentence structures that may or may not create writer's voice and tone appropriate to audience	Sufficient control of grammar, mechanics, spelling, usage, and sentence formation
2	No apparent point but evidence of a specific topic	Limited content with inadequate elaboration or explanation	Confused or inconsistent arrangement of content with or without attempts at transition	Limited word choice and control of sentence structures that inhibit voice and tone	Limited control of grammar, mechanics, spelling, usage, and sentence formation
1	Minimal evidence of a topic	Superficial and/or minimal content	Minimal control of content arrangement	Minimal variety in word choice and minimal control of sentence structures	Minimal control of grammar, mechanics, spelling, usage, and sentence formation

Nonscorable	Off-Prompt
• Is illegible; i.e., includes so many indecipherable words that no sense can be made of the response • Is incoherent; i.e., words are legible but syntax is so garbled that response makes no sense • Is insufficient; i.e., does not include enough to assess domains adequately • Is a blank paper	• Is readable but did not respond to prompt

Appendix 4–B

Feature Article Rubric

Points	Headline	Lead	Organization/Style	Content	Primary Sources Photos and/or Documents
5	summarizes the article; not written in a sentence but must include a noun and action verb	lead establishes an angle that is maintained throughout the story; hooks the reader with an interesting and relevant story, quote, statistic/ or strong visual image	uses essay format with a clear and definite beginning, middle, and end; colorful, descriptive, and vivid words are used throughout the story; article contains flawless mechanics and sophisticated transitions	accurately reflects the viewpoint of the hometown newspaper; has accurate and relevant information; and shows thought, effort, and creativity	has excellent and relevant image(s) with caption(s)
3-4	present	lead hooks reader but not in using one of the level-five strategies	article is organized, but the ideas do not flow smoothly; some colorful language and transitions are present, but they are not sophisticated; demonstrates some weaknesses in mechanics, affecting readability of article	article mainly reflects the viewpoint of the hometown newspaper; has accurate and relevant information; and shows thought, effort, and creativity	has good and relevant image(s) with caption(s)
1-2	present	lead does not give not give the reader a clear idea of the direction of the article	article is not well organized; ideas do not flow; no colorful language and transitions are weak; many errors in mechanics	article somewhat reflects the viewpoint of the hometown newspaper. lacks relevant/accurate information; and shows little thought, effort, and creativity	image has little relevance and no caption
0	not present	not clear or not present	article is not organized or comprehensible	article does not reflect the viewpoint of the hometown newspaper and is inaccurate	not present
Your Score multiplied by 3					
Total Score and Letter Grade for News Story and Photo Work					

Appendix 4-C

*Feature Story Rubric

Student Name: _____ Story slug: _____

CRITERIA	Cub reporter	Rookie	Page editor	Prize winner
PURPOSE/AUDIENCE: The degree to which the writer maintains a clear purpose to communicate with the reader by: *focusing content *using a form of a feature story to inform/entertain (personality profile, narrative, news feature, etc.) *addressing the informational needs of the reader so reader knows story's purpose early on	Limited awareness of audience with no obvious use of the characteristics of a feature article (Ex. written in Dear Diary format or inappropriate chronological order)	Some evidence of purpose and focus on audience. Some characteristics of feature story, but may be incorrectly or inconsistently used	Story is focused on purpose communicated in lead. Has "hook" and keeps reader's needs in mind. Has characteristics of feature story appropriate for topic. Story is interesting and informative.	In addition, story has strong awareness of reader needs by successfully communicating information in interesting manner. Story reads well from beginning to end with a high level of reader engagement.
IDEA DEVELOPMENT/SUPPORT: The degree to which the writer develops and supports main ideas and deepens audience understanding by using: *accurate, well-researched details. *direct and/or indirect quotations *objective reporting that avoids reporter bias *absence of libel	Little idea development, no research-based information; obvious bias and/or personal information; no quotes of any kind	Ideas are there, but remain unelaborated or disjointed. Few or poorly written quotations. Little or weak research. Few or uninteresting details.	Ideas are developed. Direct and/or indirect quotations support idea development, but may be general. There is evidence of research, but it is not well focused on main ideas.	In addition, depth of idea development supported by well-researched content, quotations and interesting details. Appropriate use of quotations. Details are specific and support main focus.
ORGANIZATION: The degree to which the writer creates unity and coherence to accomplish the purpose by: *engaging the audience in the lead and establishing a context for reading *using transitions to smoothly guide the reader through the story through the beginning, middle and end	Random and or weak organization; no or inappropriate attempt to engage audience in lead; no transitions; ideas leap-frog from one to another	Lapses in organization and coherence with some evidence of planning. May have a good lead but lacks flow. Uses some of the characteristics of a feature article.	Logical, coherent organization with attention to audience informational needs throughout story. Story has beginning, middle, end, and has characteristics of a feature article appropriate for the topic.	In addition, logical and coherent organization enables story to flow from beginning to end. Transitions are used appropriately and weave story parts together seamlessly.
SENTENCES/LANGUAGE/CORRECTNESS: The degree to which the writer creates effective and correct sentences that: *are varied in structure and length *are constructed effectively and correctly *have strong verbs and avoid passive *have documentation and correct attribution *define difficult terms, avoid slang *use AP and/or school style	Sentences incorrect in structure or ineffective; may have many errors that prevent communication of ideas; no effort to attribute information; inappropriate use of slang, profanity	Simplistic sentences may be repetitive or vague. Some technical errors do not interfere with meaning. Sources have some attribution. Major or frequent style errors.	Sentences are effective, correct and varied; have few errors in spelling, punctuation, grammar or AP style. Most sources are documented appropriately.	In addition, sentences have emotional impact and are information rich. Story has few or no errors in spelling or style. Writing has strong verbs and is lively and engaging.
SOURCES: Student has interview questions and notes that demonstrate good communication skills with sources: *questions are open-ended *variety of sources appropriate for story *notes are fairly legible and complete	No questions or notes turned in. No apparent use of interview.	Questions may be "yes-no" type. Sources may be inappropriate or too limited. Notes may be legible but are sketchy, incomplete. Notes may not match contents of story.	Questions show depth of understanding. Sources are appropriate for story. Story reflects meaningful notes in length and content.	In addition, questions get at the "story behind the story." Notes are complete and reveal descriptions as well as quotations, background as well as narration or summary.

Jackie Bretz, MJE, Western Kentucky University

Appendix 4–D

The Life of George Robertson: A Mother's Worst Fear

By: Nathan Close

Just after receiving orders for my next mission, I realized what I was getting myself into. *I can't believe I'm actually going to be bombing Hanoi… It's OK; I've been preparing my whole career for this moment. All my hours of hard work and training come down to this mission.* Then the thought hit me… *I might die…*

George Andrew Robertson Jr. was born on March 23, 1946, in Wilkinsburg, PA to Martha McCaskie and George Andrew Robertson Sr. His childhood excluded such luxuries as computers, jet engines, MRI's, and ex-rays, some of which, when created, helped generate his career path. Growing up, he and his brothers – Walter and the late Dale – loved trains. Each boy had a set, and, along with their father, each played with them incessantly. Later in his childhood, George eventually moved on to tricycles and bicycles.

Growing up as a teenager, George and a group of friends had an open field in which they played football, baseball, and everything they could think of. He later began working at a local country club, first as a caddie and eventually as Caddie Master. Upon completing High School, George made his way to Westminster College. He finished his college career with a BA in Business and Economics. Westminster was also where George met Kristin, his spouse of 11 years.

On June 5, 1969, George Robertson joined the Air force, in order to help serve in the Vietnam War. When asked why the Air force, he responded simply "I didn't want to carry a rifle!" In the Air force, George served as a pilot, a maintenance supervisor, a safety investigator, and eventually a test and evaluation planner. While these all provided

Appendix 4–D *continued*

self-satisfaction, camaraderie, and entertainment, they occasionally delivered a brief fright or two. For instance, George recalls once having his airplane go off the runway, and another time experiencing a vertigo. Following George's tour of duty in Vietnam, he decided to continue the Air force as a career.

During George's 21 years of Air force service, he was stationed in Texas, Mississippi, California, Guam, Vietnam, and Virginia. He enjoyed his stay in California from 1972-1981 the best. While in Saigon, Vietnam, George was stationed at Ton Son Nhut Airbase. While serving in Saigon, Robertson flew the Goonybird - an old World War II airplane code named the DC-3 and EC-47. He also helped his squadron with electronic reconnaissance and surveillance. Communication, however, was different then. Since e-mail was not yet created, everything George did to communicate was through the mail. He could send letters or cassette tapes, and in return could receive packages, and even once some broken Girl Scout Cookies sent by his sister, Martha.

George was born the first child, with 2 brothers and one sister. Dale was born second, then Walter, and finally Martha. Dale died when he was five of cancer. Martha was born after his death, so she never knew him. George was already 11 years old – a preteen – at the time of Martha's birth. Born with lots of aunts and uncles on both sides, George never had a shortage of ears to listen to him.

George's last assignment with the Air force brought him to Virginia to work on a special project at the Pentagon. Years after retiring from the Air force, George remains at the Pentagon working as a civilian doing projects in Test and Evaluation for the Secretary of the Air force.

Appendix 4–D *continued*

George currently resides in his home in Herndon, Virginia, along with his wife of over 21 years, Judy Nicodemus. He enjoys visiting with his stepdaughter, Jenny, in Albany, New York, and "playing golf and sleeping;" just ask his wife or mother. George also belongs to the Daedaliens – a fraternity for heavier than air pilots – which helps collect money for scholarships, and promotes all things about aviation. He loves watching NFL Football on TV the most, though golf comes in a close second. Upon retirement from the Pentagon, George wishes to teach his nephew to golf, and even caddie for him if he makes the Professional Golf Association Tour. (PGA Tour)

Even though George had frightening experiences while in Vietnam, he returned with all well. He came back with his pride intact, and his priorities straight. He remains a hero to many, including me, and a down-to-earth uncle, brother, husband, son, father, and friend. Although some may envy George's accomplishments, he remains humble and prefers hard work to boasting.

Appendix 4—E Reflection Sheet

Chapter 4: Feature Article

What is my response to the opening thoughts and questions (*in italics*)?

What was the most valuable information that I gained personally and/or for my classroom?

What do I still need to know more about? Where could I go to get that information?

What ideas can I add to what I've already learned?

Memoir

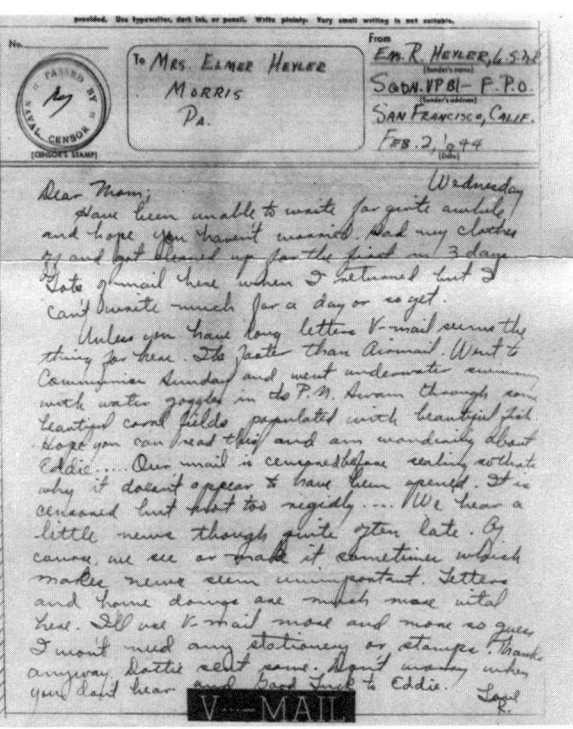

Figure 5–1 Letters home from World War II, V mail (Victory mail) from a son to his mother are authentic memoirs of that time.

Think about some possible artifacts, events, or people that helped to shape your literacy growth and awareness of family historical and cultural influences. Write them down and then think about your relationship to them. How did they influence your life? Why are they important to you?

A few years ago, when I began the process of researching and writing for my master's thesis, an interpretative work about the works of William Faulkner and Eudora Welty, I decided to interview my mother and my aunts about a family story that influenced their own way of telling stories. As I began searching for an example of memoir to show my students, I returned to a part of my thesis and rediscovered the following:

> After hearing two versions of the same story, I decided that it really would be best to contact the third and eldest aunt, who was living in a retirement community in Florida. Aunt Marian, a born storyteller, immediately offered that it had been years since she'd thought of this bit of family history and that anymore she "got things in her history muddled up with Wilbur's (her deceased husband) side of the family." Nevertheless, she thought a moment, then began a third version. This time her great-grandfather Burley took his son Well's place in the war. He did this to ensure that if he were killed the young man would take care of the mother. Steve Mudge, maybe that was the name, a cousin of her father, also enlisted in the regiment, and "Uncle Steve was the youngest in the regiment and Grandfather Burley was the oldest." She recalled that Steve was a tall man—six feet, six inches tall. Both men were captured and sent to Southern prisons, although she was not sure if they were in the same prison or not. Again, though, she told how Grandfather Burley nearly starved in Andersonville, and now, on his way North, he had overeaten and died. Although this aunt did not offer to continue the story of Martin Mudge, she did offer insight on why the stories were different. "Ten years kind of filtered the story out of my mind, but you know that the Indians [Native Americans] lived together and that's how they kept their stories correct and going through the years." As my aunt indicated, the value of oral tradition—so integral to Native American peoples—is rapidly fading in mainstream American culture.

Three women, all sisters who grew up in the same house deep in the mountains of northern Pennsylvania, told versions of the story I recalled from my youth. On each telling, the differences became startling. Of this I am sure: two men, one from my grandfather's family and one from my grandmother's family, went to the Civil War. One was a very old man, and one was a young man. Both enlisted in the same regiment, both went to prison; one man died while returning, while the other somehow made it home. That is the core of the tale, but the additions, the subtractions, the reliance on memory, and the distrust of memory all make three distinct recollections united by a central event. Although this is basically the story I remember as a youth, I remember the tellers offering more physical descriptions, more specific family names, more geographical locations, and generally, more detail. Yet each version was given as the truth by the women; although they allowed for memory failings and admonished that it would be best to check with others, what they told was the truth for them and a possibility of truth for those who listened.

I presented a portion of this document to my eighth-grade class. My hope was to show them the workings of memory that lead into a memoir. During a discussion about the piece and the workings of memory, one student raised her hand and said, "But, if you wrote this, and it is about a story you know and your family . . . well . . . then isn't this your memoir?"

Memoir

The memoir is an integral part of the Oral History Project in that it moves away from the factual information of research and feature article and invites the subject to have a voice in the project. In fact, voice becomes an important element of the project. Using information generated from the interview, research, and artifacts, the student assembles a memoir that not only relates an incident from the life of the subject but also shows how that event, person, or artifact helped to shape the subject's life.

In short, the memoir is an anecdotal story of the subject's life. It may revolve around a memory, experience, or time period. It may be about a person, or it could be about an artifact from the subject's life. In most instances, the memoir is written by the subject and presented by the student; however, there are times when this is not the case. The memoir can also be written by the student, be written by the student and the participant together, or be transcribed by the student from a recording. No matter the scenario, the purpose of the memoir is essentially to relate a narrative that re-

CD Connection

Go to Main Menu and click on Gallery. Scroll down to News Article Module; Video - Teacher Introduces The Memoir Assignment To His Class.

volves around artifacts and to show some form of influence or shape on the participant's life.

Memoir writing not only relays facts and happenings about the participant's life, it also allows students to become reflective. In writing their own memoirs and reading the memoirs of the participants, students have the opportunity to become more reflective about history, the lives of participants, and ultimately their own lives. They are afforded the chance to read narratives of others and discover similarities in experiences and feelings. Memoirs work not only on the academic level of the writing process, but also on a level of human connection (Figure 5–2).

When first instructing in how to write memoirs, it is important to discuss or include a definition of memoir. We begin by reading the definition from a dictionary and establishing that a memoir is a memory of one person; that person becomes the protagonist and has an important part in the story.

At this point it is important to review narrative writing and to show how narrative writing is different from the other forms we use most: informative (expository) and persuasive.

Figure 5–2 Kittie Belle Hubbard Mudge, 1880–1967 Tioga County, Pennsylvania. What might this lady's story be?

Because the memoir to be written for the oral history project may be done in several forms and the student will be working with the subject on the final memoir, one way to practice memoir writing is to have each student write an actual memoir from his or her own perspective. One method that works well is the "Name Story." Often students have difficulty coming up with memoirs because they live in such a fast-paced world that they often remember fleeting events, or their artifacts may be something from the current media. All students have a name; therefore, many students find this activity an accessible way to begin writing their memoirs.

Name Story

Students write their full name on a piece of paper. Underneath their full name they begin asking questions about their name.

Example

What is my first name?

What is my last name?

Who named me?

Who else has my last name?

What does my name remind me of?

What does my name literally mean?

Who was I named after?

What family stories are associated with my name? Are there other stories?

Where did my name come from?

Has my name been passed on from other people?

There are a host of other questions that will result in answers about the students' names. By modeling the questions about your own name on the board or the overhead and jotting the answers beside the questions, students soon are onto their own prewriting and generating questions about their names. Many students know some information about their names; some students look up the literal meaning of their names, and nearly all students will seek more personal information about their names from their parents and grandparents. It's important to pose the question, "How has my name affected me?" This final question will serve to shape the memoir and give it meaning to the student.

Once we have generated questions and compiled information about the names, it is time to begin writing the memoir. The name serves as the artifact, and the questions generated during prewriting are now the content of the text.

As memoir writing is narrative writing, we return to our information about narrative to guide us in creating the rough draft. Using the questions, students then write the story of how they received their names and how this particular name has affected their lives. Sometimes the stories are humorous, sometimes they are moving, but always they are interesting. Even the students who repeat, "I hate my name; it is boring," return to the class with information about their names. Nearly every student can relate a time when his name has been an important force in life.

Once the draft is finished, we revise, and then publish our name memoirs. All students have then written their own memoir and are ready to move on to the memoir of the project.

Student Memoirs

Another method of introducing students to writing a memoir is to have them work through the actual process but only letting them choose the artifact, event, or person about which to write. Again, model an artifact, and then use questions to generate a prewriting about the artifact.

Teacher Example
Years ago I was given a shaving mirror that belonged to my grandfather. This particular mirror predates the American Civil War and was used by my grandfather until he died in 1950. It was given to my mother, who then gave it to me, aside from a few photographs it is the only tangible item I have that once belonged to my grandfather. I bring the mirror into the classroom, present it to the class, and begin, either on the board or on the overhead, to ask questions.

> What does the mirror look like?
>
> Who gave me the mirror?
>
> Who originally had the mirror?

How did I come to possess it?

How do I use the mirror?

What stories do I have about it?

When did I receive it?

Where was it before I had it?

What memories do I have of this mirror?

What people do I associate with this?

How has this mirror influenced my life?

Once I have generated questions about the mirror and have responded to them, students are then charged to think of a list of artifacts, events, or people who have left lasting impressions on their lives. Encourage students to generate a list first; it is easier then to choose from a list than it is to pick only one item. Brainstorming artifacts, events, and people will lead to a rich list, which will lead to a memoir that will be important to the student. This will help students see that the goal of memoir writing is to investigate a memory that will add meaning to our lives.

When students have finished brainstorming and each student has a list, it is time to select one item from the list and, using that item, construct a prewriting that will give them enough information to write the memoir. Using the basic *who, what, when, where, why,* and *how* questions, students can generate much information about their items and have material for their resultant memoirs. The student example in Figure 5–3 shows how one student, Maggie, used those questions to begin guiding her through writing her grandfather's memoir.

Writing the Student Memoir

As students begin to write the drafts of the memoirs, consider the assessment of the piece. Our particular areas of assessment are focus, organization, content, style, and conventions.

Focus
Students are encouraged to select one item from their brainstorming list for their prewriting and are then encouraged to write about this item and how it affected their lives. By adhering to the narrative struc-

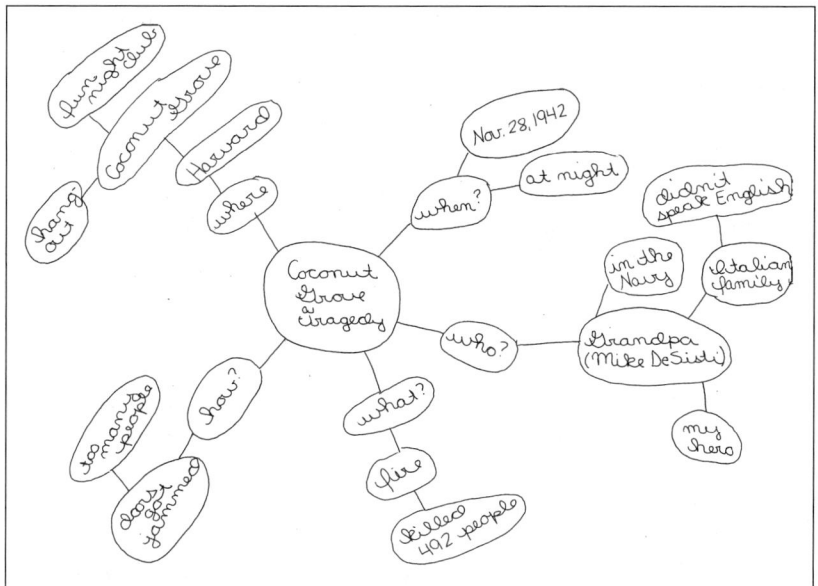

Figure 5–3 Maggie's first prewrite.

ture, and concentrating on one item and its story, we avoid confusing memoir with autobiography. Although these two types of writing are similar, the autobiography tends to be wide in scope and encompasses the entire life. The memoir focuses on *one* aspect of the writer's life and the meaning it brings to that life; the memoir shows what the writer has learned from this experience. Also by focusing on the narrative mode, we stay away from more informational/expository writing, which also tends to be wider in scope, and it is easier to stick to one part of the writer's life. Our focus is to probe an artifact, event, or person for how it relates to the subject's life and to show what the writer learned from the experience.

Organization
Like most narrative forms, the memoir has a beginning, middle, and end. By using this structure, the writer avoids merely listing facts and happenings in the writer's life. Also, by using this type of organization, the writer can put structure to what otherwise might be a confusing attempt to sort out meaning from memory. For example, one student related how he was afraid when his brother joined the army, but then his brother left him with a football—the main artifact—and kept corresponding with him while he was in the army. The student

wrote about clinging to the football because it belonged to his brother, but as time went on and his brother wrote and talked to him more about how "safe" he really was, he gradually used the football in play and at home; instead of protecting it, he used it. He ended the memoir by writing how he let go of his fear and learned to use the artifact and therefore grew up a bit more. The structure had a decided beginning, middle, and end, and the memoir became his favorite piece of writing for that year.

Content

Through brainstorming activities, students come up with appropriate content for the memoir, and most students, once settled on an idea and a focus, are ready to begin. It is important to take some time and explore how to generate and use appropriate details in the memoir. Details help the reader to feel as if she is actually there in the events of the story. By using descriptions, anecdotes, names, dates, quotes, and more exact details, students learn to put an abstract idea into concrete terms and let the reader into the story. One student wrote about his move from a rural area to our more suburban school. He missed the forest behind his house where he used to play and hike. On first writing about life there, he referred to the forest as "the woods behind my house" and gave no more details. After brainstorming and a bit of revising, the forest became, "the muddy trails that lead around maple, ash, and a few scattered oak trees. Squirrels played in the limbs that hung over a small creek, and my brother and I ran through the cold water of the creek, to a fort we had built deeper in the woods." Suddenly the details invited both the reader and the writer to explore the memory and see how the transition from country life to town life had been a difficult transition.

Coupled with details is the attention to and use of sensory details. By using sensory details the writer can help the reader to see, hear, touch, taste, and smell details and events in the memoir. The same writer referring to the move from the country not only wrote about the deep green leaves of the maple trees and the cold, fresh taste of the creek water, but he also mentioned the acrid smell of the pavement in town and the sound of cars whooshing down his new street replacing the "caw" of the crow in the fields surrounding his country house. It wasn't until we revised his work that his use of sensory details begin to liven his memoir, making it more immediate and meaningful to the reader.

Another method of supplying details that create more vivid and exact writing is to *show* and *not tell* when giving information. One sentence in the country-to-town memoir read, "I was always afraid when night came and I was still in the woods." After working on that sentence during a peer-revising session, the new sentence read, "If I stayed too late in the woods and the darkness began to come in, I thought I could hear sounds behind every tree. My skin prickled, and I kept looking behind me as the wind moaned in the tree limbs."

Sometimes, a prewriting or brainstorm will need to be revisited to help with details because writing is recursive. One student, Maggie, found her prewriting about her grandfather had only "started" the process; she realized that she needed to rethink what she had done and add to her prewriting. With some guidance and attention to details she revised her first prewriting (Figure 5–4). Now Maggie's prewriting had details to begin a vivid memoir. (See Appendix 5–A for the memoir Maggie wrote about her grandfather, "Coconut Grove Fire Tragedy").

One more detail to encourage students to use is direct quotations. It is easy to learn through reading memoirs and other stories, both fiction and nonfiction, that using people's exact words is an efficient and interesting way to let them speak. By using people's actual words, stu-

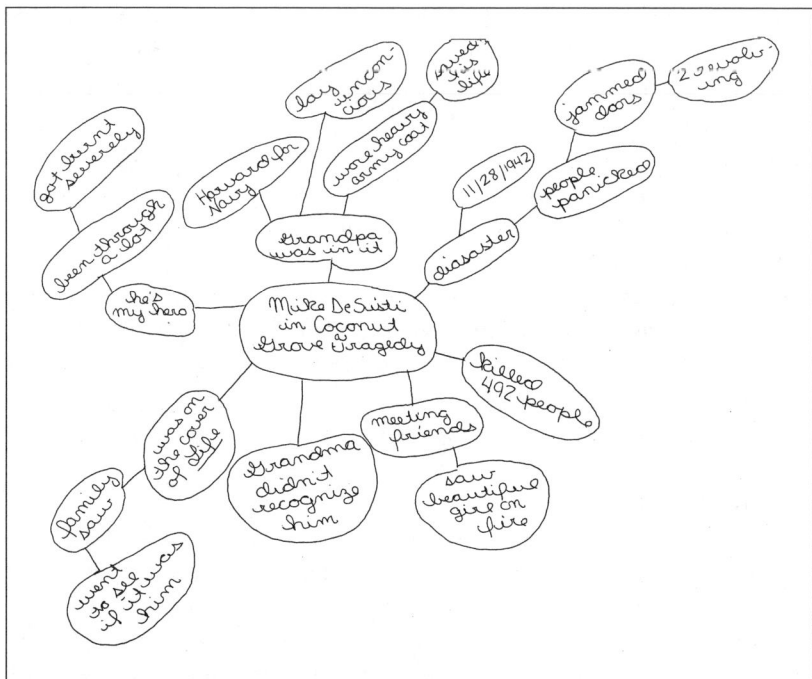

Figure 5–4 Maggie's second prewrite.

dents not only are using what was actually said but adding honest emotions and voice to the story.

One particular memoir of a student quoted his grandmother about the Vietnam War: "My grandma said, 'We wrote to him often but he almost never wrote back. Sometimes we even got so scared something had happened to him that we called the Red Cross to make sure that he was ok. During those terrible six years I was even scared to answer the door for fear the army was there to tell me he wasn't coming home.'" Through the use of his grandmother's exact words, suddenly the memory of his grandmother becomes immediate and she is in front of the reader, relating her part in this memoir.

As they brainstorm, write, and revise, students keep alert for details. They know that using details is the difference between flat, dull writing where the reader is not pulled in and exciting, crisp, vivid writing where the reader is not only invited into the story but becomes a witness to the events and can more readily understand how the memory affected the writer and the writer's life.

Style
The writer uses style, specifically varying sentence structures and attending to strong word choice, to create a tone in the work. Tone becomes important to the memoir, as it is one more way to engage the reader. The student writing about his grandmother as a person who was important to and affected his life created a tone of strength. Each detail he chose lent itself to creating a portrait of strength, which eventually had to overcome the fear a mother felt when a son was at war. This student structured his sentences to emphasize the fear his grandmother felt: "For her it was one of the scariest times of her life as a mother, her son was sent to Vietnam." By choosing words wisely and structuring sentences for the proper effect, it is possible for the student to do something sophisticated in writing—create tone. This tone can be comic, fearful, happy, tragic, sad, scary, and the whole range of emotions that make up the events in life.

Conventions
The conventions of student's writing are actually the steps attended to toward the end of this process. Many students, if not directed, will use revising to clean up conventions—usage, spelling, mechanics, grammar problems—instead of attending to minor mistakes in the editing stage. When writing and revising, it is important to concentrate on the first four steps—*focus, organization, content,* and *style*—in order to

create a coherent, moving piece of writing that becomes the memoir. Proofreading, an important step where editing occurs, takes place just before the final copy and before the final act of publishing.

Preparing for the Subject's Memoir

After writing their own memoirs, most students are more aware of the importance and characteristics of memoir writing. After reading examples of memoirs and writing their own, it is time to brainstorm and with a bit of guidance arrive at the following characteristics of the memoir.

- It evolves from an artifact, event, or person.
- It is a memory of something that happened in the past.
- It combines narrative writing with descriptive writing.
- It has meaning for the writer; it displays what the writer has learned from the artifact, event, or person.
- It is different from the autobiography in that it focuses on *one* item.

It is during these discussions of characteristics that you move into the purpose for the memoir—giving meaning to an event and giving voice to the Oral History Project. Have your students begin to focus on creating their subject's memoir. With instruction about the framework and mechanics of the memoir, it is time to return to the interview to prepare to elicit the memory from the subject.

Students, once prepared for the interview, generate questions and directions for the interview. Spend class time designing part of the interview to center on the memoir. At the initial stages of the project, many students wanted to begin the interview by asking, "Can you think of any memoir stories?" Some of the subjects hesitated, answering in a couple of words or sentences that were brief, and although potentially rich, were unexplored. Retooling their efforts, it was decided that students needed to not only explain what the memoir was but help the subject mine for that information. That mining came through preparing for the interview, interviewing, reviewing that information, exploring artifacts, and researching.

As writing is a recursive process where one prewrites, writes, revises, prewrites more, writes more, revisits the draft, revisits the prewriting, and adds to the draft, so is this part of the Oral History

Project. Most students interview with a definite plan of what they need to accomplish; others approach in a more hit-and-miss manner. All students need to be aware of how an interview must be directed yet be flexible at the same time. Some of our most fascinating stories came from the deft student who recognized that a story was coming and that the course of the interview had changed but should not be stopped.

Students need to structure their interview with questions that will follow up a possible story. They need to probe questions about artifacts, events, and people who figured in their subject's lives. Once prepared for this, information about the memoir is much easier to compile.

Preparing the Subject's Memoir

When ready to begin preparing the subject's memoir, four methods actually work best. Although one of the methods may not technically be considered a memoir, the students do concentrate on an event, make it into a narrative, and relate the importance to the subject's life. Every student easily completes one of the following four methods.

1. The subject writes her own memoir.
2. The subject and student write the memoir together.
3. The student compiles and writes the memoir.
4. The student tapes the memoir from the subject and then transcribes it.

Each method has its own set of guidelines and pitfalls; each method, however, takes instruction and modeling. Each student and project is different, allowing for this variety allows for success in the memoir component.

The Subject Writes Her Own Memoir

Armed with the information and practice of how to write a memoir, it is time for the students to go forth and help their subjects begin their own experience writing the memoir. This first of the four methods we use tends to bring rich voice to the project and it is not a "way out" of students doing the work of the memoir. In fact, it becomes an experience in speaking and listening. Students now must take a bit of the role of teacher and guide their subjects through the experience of discovering the story behind an artifact, event, or person from their lives.

It is helpful for the student to take the artifact/memoir sheet on the initial interview visit. In the beginning of the interview process, the student has explained the Oral History Project and how the student and the subject will be going about doing the project. The best time for the student to begin explaining the memoir is toward the end of the initial interview. With the artifact/memoir sheet the student can then present the memoir to the subject and explain how to do the sheet. Sometimes students help the subject fill out the first part of the sheet, the columns asking for artifacts, events, and people. Some students even take the sheet they did in class to serve as an example. The subject may choose to work on the sheet then, with the student, or later while alone and with more time to ponder and consider their past experiences.

> **CD Connection**
>
>
>
> Go to Main Menu and click on Memoir; click on Teaching the Memoir in the left column. Click on the Gallery at the bottom of the screen and open Document - Pre-Writing Activity Blank Template.

This experience may be one of sorrow for some adults. Memories of people who have died or memories of unpleasant experiences often arise during this part of the process. Some subjects become frustrated and distressed with the process while some subjects delight in it. Always tell the students to have the subject call us at school if they become frustrated with the process. Like any learning experience, students can become frustrated also.

For those who decline to write the more troublesome memoir, encourage them to try another artifact, and this is the time to explain that nearly everything in life has its story, and that students must remember these stories and show how they influenced their lives. It is also helpful for the student to share her own classroom memoir with the subject. With an example before them, many adults begin to launch into their own story.

Another troublesome situation may arise—the subject may feel his writing abilities are inferior. Each year students report that "my grandma wants to write her own memoir, but she doesn't want people to see that she doesn't write well and can't spell," or, "my neighbor didn't go past eighth grade; he'd like to write his memoir, he just doesn't want people to laugh at his writing skills."

At this point you can show students how their skills in peer conferencing can be used. Students can read the memoir back to the subject—the way it was written—and then the subject can begin any revisions. Coach students to be kind and patient with their subjects during this component; coach them to be as patient as they would like adults to be with them. They must listen to the subjects and be able to communicate about the subject's success in writing. At the same time, they are showing the subject how to revise to help the writing.

As for editing a piece, many subjects have their own computers with spelling and grammar checks. If not, our students can serve as proofreaders for the piece, so when it is published on the triptych, it is as error-free as possible.

Some subjects have even selected to handwrite their final copy memoir to be published on the triptych. Many touching memoirs appear in the script of the subject. This has double advantages. First, it includes the voice of the subject in the form of the memoir; second, it introduces a bit of intimacy that the printed word lacks. The physical script as well and the words of the subject are now part of this historical record. Like finding that handwritten letter in a box in an attic, now a letter imbued with voice and effort becomes a part of the project. Students have been especially proud of such handwritten memoirs.

Subject and Student Write the Memoir Together

Not all oral history subjects are eager to write their memoirs, and some students need a bit of guidance in doing the project. This form of memoir writing, where the subject and the student actually collaborate and write the memoir together, allows the student to actually use the writing process to create a piece of writing, allows the subject more time with the student and to use the student's expertise in memoir writing, and allows two people to come together in a synergistic manner to probe the memoir.

As with the first method of memoir writing, the student goes forth equipped with all the tools for writing the memoir. Possessing information garnered from the interview and any possible research, the student can now return to the subject and begin the collaboration process.

With encouragement from the teacher, at the subject's home, at a predetermined place such as a library or community center, or at school, the student can begin to compile the information. Encourage students to begin with the questions that might elicit memoir-type information. The artifact/memoir sheet is good to take to this part of the collaboration. Once the two—subject and student—fill out the sheet, with the student guiding the partner, recommend moving onto prewriting to pull the information about *one* experience together. Maggie's prewriting (see Figure 5–4 on p. 97) about her grandfather was actually completed by both Maggie and her grandfather.

Once the prewriting is complete, it is time to move into a first draft. Moving through a webbing or a prewriting for a subject who has been out of school for thirty or more years could be a formidable task. For today's students, prewriting and drafting are a known part of the process; therefore, collaborating brings together two worlds: the world of the student, who is familiar with the writing process, and the world of the subject, who has many rich stories of her life's experiences.

The student and the participant now create their draft, using the memoir guidelines from the class:

Narrative Structure
- beginning
- middle
- end
- purpose
- one event, artifact, person
- dialogue where needed

Once a draft is finished, the student can return to the classroom, conference with the teacher, and return to revise with the participant as necessary. Encourage students to return with the draft to let the participant read it once more for any changes in style or content. As students are encouraged to revise to make writing more accurate, the participant and student are encouraged to do the same. Many times, in the period between visits, participants have remembered more details to add to the memoir, thus giving it more depth, accuracy, and voice.

The Student Compiles and Writes the Memoir

Not every subject is inclined to write her own memoir. When this arises, we encourage the student to become the memoirist for the participant. Like a biographer, the student, after the interview and proper research, has accumulated information to compile and write a memoir for the subject. Again, we stress that this is not an "autobiography" or the complete life story of an individual. This is *one* narrative of a special event, artifact, or person in the subject's life.

CD Connection

Go to Main Menu and click on Gallery. Scroll down to Memoir Module, Video - Writing A Memoir For Your Interviewee.

In this scenario, the student prepares by conducting the initial interview, does follow-up research, and then works with the subject to finish the artifact/memoir sheet. Once this is done, the student has an idea of what areas will lend themselves to creating the memoir.

To successfully do this form of memoir writing, the student would need to do a subsequent interview, one especially devoted to generating a memoir. After generating questions about a couple of the work page ideas, the student can then return for another session with the subject. Now the questions deal with what artifact, event, or person is the subject going to talk about and what influence this has had on the subject's life. Either by writing down the information, taping the interview, or doing a combination of both, the student now has the basic information to structure the memoir.

Upon returning to the classroom, we advise the student to take the information and do a draft in order to begin compiling the information and discovering the basic structure. Once the draft is complete and the student feels he has enough information to begin, it is time for the first draft. When a student chooses this form of writing a memoir, the use of third person becomes the strongest point of view. Using *he, she,* or the person's name not only shows that the subject did not pen this work but it also allows the student to combine factual information from the subject with narrative skills from the classroom. With the point of view established, it is time to use the prewriting and the memoir questions to create the draft.

It is important that the student be accurate and honest with the information and create a memoir that truly reflects the story told by the subject. After creating this narrative with a beginning, middle, and end that is a memory of one piece of life, it is best if the student returns to the subject and works with the subject to revise the draft. This ensures the subject can assess the memoir for accuracy and details. Now the subject, upon reading the story, may have more information to share, details to correct, and other information to change. No one wants to read a triptych of an important instance in his life and discover wrong information or other surprises.

This process, when a student actually pens the memoir for the adult, is a time when the student actually has two audiences and works to make the best possible piece. One audience is the crowd of adults and students who will visit the Oral History Fair or sit in the classroom; but the other, more immediate audience, is the actual subject. This audience is immediate, real, and frequently involved in the life of the student. Memoir writing by the students is often very heartfelt. They are engaged in the story of this person and they make this story as clear, accurate, and interesting as possible.

Student Tapes the Memoir From the Subject and Then Transcribes It

The final method we use to produce a memoir is to rely on the time-honored method of doing oral history, and that is to tape the memoir from the subject and then to transcribe it into document form for publishing with the project. Students tend to have fun with this form as they get to use the tape recorder and actually conduct the interview as a professional would. In fact, many students protect their taped interview with more vigilance than their handwritten interview. The taped memoir, however, presents its own set of successes and problems, and it has its own procedure.

When gathering interview questions and research prior to the initial interview, advise students to have the Artifact/Memoir Sheet ready for the interview. When they are prepared with the memoir page, they can steer their subject toward the beginning thoughts of the memoir. Thus both the interviewer and the subject are thinking about relating one particular story from the past. Advise the student to return to a session with the subject when the memoir is the focus. Like the interview, this session can be done in the home of the subject or the interviewer, a neutral location, or even at school. Once they have worked through the Artifact/Memoir Sheet and are ready to begin, the taping can start.

It is important for students to have the tape recorder ready, with a set of fresh batteries and extra tapes if needed. They have been trained in correct use of taping, so they are not "sticking" the recorder in an obtrusive place and hampering the storytelling. Once the student has settled on one or two ideas from the artifact/memoir sheet, she can direct the subject into relating an incident about the artifact, person, or event. The stories told tend to unfold naturally with only a bit of prompting by the student. Once you get past the "Oh, I don't have any stories to tell" stage, we find that all the subjects actually do have stories to tell, and some have many stories to tell.

After recording a story or two, the student then returns to the classroom where the transcribing begins. This can be a daunting and sometimes problematic task. Some students don't want to transcribe every word; moreover, they find that listening to the recorder and trying to copy down the words is actually quite time-consuming. Some students prefer to type the conversation while transcribing, and some rely on handwriting to get down the words. Most students run into garbled words, faint and inaudible sentences and phrases. Nearly all students play certain passages over and over until they feel they have the words correctly.

Stress to your students to copy all the words down in the story, unless the subject repeats the same phrases over and over. Students will quickly discover that people do not speak in complete sentences, they do not tell stories chronologically, they repeat themselves, they do not speak in public school grammar, and they tell fascinating and even moving stories. Stressing clarity and accuracy in the transcribing is important, as you don't want students putting in their own wording when they want to take a shortcut and finish the task for the tape recorder. It is important to create a memoir that is told by the subject. Otherwise, the words are "interpreted" by the students.

Once the transcribing has taken place, the final product can be produced in several ways, but use two distinct formats. For the first method let the students present the memoir in the "interviewer–interviewee" format. The interviewer is labeled and the typed question is then presented; then the answer is presented and labeled with the subject's name. This format is familiar to most students as it is frequently used in magazines popular with teens and newspapers often use this method.

Example of Interviewer–Interviewee

Interviewer: Well, what can you tell me about the story your sister told me? You know the one about your ancestors being at Andersonville Prison during the Civil War?

Aunt Marian: Oh, that old story. Well, you know, sometimes I get this history all muddled up in my mind.

Interviewer: I do that myself. And I'll bet you remember at least part of the story.

Aunt Marian: I remember that Pa always said that it was his grandfather Burley, and he took his son's place in the war. People used to do that then. He did this to ensure that if he got killed, the young man would take care of the mother.

Interviewer: Much different than today.

Aunt Marian: I guess so. Well Uncle Steve was the youngest in the regiment and Grandfather Burley was the oldest. I even remember Uncle Steve. He was a tall man—six feet and six inches tall. Well, both men were captured and sent to Southern prisons, hmmm . . . I'm not sure if they were in the same prison, but I know that one of them was in Andersonville. That was the worst of all the prisons.

Interviewer: Do you know about their life inside the prison?

Aunt Marian: Only what I've read, Pa and Uncle Steve never really talked about them. But I know that Grandfather Burley nearly starved when he was in prison. He lived there for . . . oh . . . hmmm . . . probably over a year. When he came home, you know, on his way back to the North. Now, if I remember right, it was in South Carolina, no, maybe it was in Philadelphia. Anyway, somewhere after he was let go, he overate. You know, somebody who was trying to help out. And that killed him.

The next format is to present the transcribed text in block form with breaks for paragraphs. This is the story transcribed from the tapes without the interrupting questions. Students frequently want to rearrange the material to make a "perfect" chronological fit and they want to clean up the grammar and be creative with punctuation. Most times, when the material is transcribed, students go back to listen to the tape with their typed copy and find that they don't need to be creative with wording or punctuation, for the natural breaks of people while telling their stories provide them with the proper punctuation. If chronological problems do occur, the student, with the subject, must ultimately make the decision.

Example of Block Method of Memoir Transcription

Interviewer: Well, what can you tell me about the story your sister told me? You know the one about your ancestors being at Andersonville Prison during the Civil War?

Aunt Marian: Oh, that old story. Well, you know, sometimes I get this history all muddled up in my mind. I remember that Pa always said that it was his grandfather Burley, and he took his son's place in the war. People used to do that then. He did this to ensure that if he got killed, the young man would take care of the mother. I guess so. Well, Uncle Steve was the youngest in the regiment and Grandfather Burley was the oldest. I even remember Uncle Steve. He was a tall man—six feet and six inches tall. Well both men were captured and sent to Southern prisons, hmm . . . I'm not sure if they were in the same prison, but I know that one of them was in Andersonville. That was the worst of all the prisons. Only what I've read, Pa and Uncle Steve never really talked about them. But I know that Grandfather Burley nearly starved when he was in prison. He lived there for . . . oh . . . hmm . . . probably over a year. When he came home, you know, on his way back to the North. Now, if I remember right, it was in South Carolina, no, maybe it was in Philadelphia. Anyway, somewhere after he was let go, he overate. You know somebody who was trying to help out. And that killed him.

Students return with the finished transcribed memoir to their subjects so they can read it, and then both the student and subject can revise together. After all, they are still using the subject's words and ideas. This last revision will nearly always result in changes in chronology and the memoir becomes stronger. Also, upon time away from the interview, subjects remember more details, can check spellings of names, and can check the story for accuracy. By doing this, both are using the revision process to make the memoir stronger.

Bylines

When publishing the final project, encourage the students to have their byline immediately after the title. As there are four methods of writing the memoir, there are four types of bylines to be used. Each one is different and alludes to how the memoir was written. Most people know it is the story of the subject, but now the memoir writing gets its ownership.

The subject writes the memoir.	Written by (subject's name)
The subject and student write the memoir.	Written by (subject's and student's name)
The student compiles and writes the memoir.	Written by (student's name)
The student transcribes the memoir.	Transcribed by (student's name)

By using these bylines, the reader is alerted to who did the actual writing and who owns the writing of the memoir. Many subjects are proud to have written their own to be posted for the public to read, and many students are proud to add this exciting element to their project.

When it is time to assess the memoir—after all, this is an academic project—assess the initial student memoir that was written earlier in the process. You would never assess the quilting memoir of an eighty-four-year-old grandmother, neither would you assess the transcription of someone excitedly telling about meeting JFK. The student's personal stories serve the purpose of practicing the narrative form. Students have found that their own memoir writing helps them when they need to guide their subjects into creating the memoirs. The students know the format and can give guidance and assistance to elicit a well-written memoir.

During the memoir component one concept that enters nearly all memoirs is dialogue. Emphasize that letting people's actual words onto the page and into the narrative gives the memoir power and a stronger voice. Whether collaborating with the subject or transcribing the subject's words, all students attempt to incorporate dialogue into the memoirs. Try to instill that it won't work to merely insert quotes to take up space, but go over how by using people's actual words, a writer can convey personality, attitude, description, and a whole range of details that can vividly engage the reader and make the memoir more authentic. Students love to search for the right words that reveal the subject, but when it comes to the conventions of writing dialogue, they often get confused. Go over the following dialogue conventions with students.

- There are quotations marks around the parts that are spoken.
- The first letter of each spoken part is capitalized.
- There are dialogue tags that explain who is talking each time the speaker changes.

- A new paragraph is started after the speaker changes.
- The dialogue tags can go before, after, or in the middle of dialogue.
- The first letter of the dialogue tag is not capitalized unless it is a name or at the beginning of a sentence.
- There is always punctuation—a comma, a period, a question mark—at the end of the spoken parts. It goes inside the quotation mark.
- There is always a period or comma at the end of the dialogue tag (Lattimer, 57).

In the initial class where students wrote their memoirs, an exercise like the following where they must supply the dialogue corrections is effective:

You can put your coat in my locker she said.
Okay I said and I'm going to put my literature book in there also. She looked at me and said no I don't want the big book to crush my lunch.
It's not going to crush your lunch I said. Then she opened her locker and I accidentally dropped my literature book on her lunch.

Students find something this short challenging and intimidating. With guidance from the teacher and consultation with partners, they can learn to apply the rules of dialogue and when the real memoir is in front of them, with actual dialogue that means something to them, they can apply what they have learned from this exercise to their own work.

One unexpected outcome of this exercise is that students will figure out where the quotation marks go and place them correctly. After that, many students will begin to notice the overuse of the word *said*. Here is an opportunity for discussion of word choice and replacing the word said with synonyms such as *whispered, squeaked, snarled, sighed, gasped, groaned, whined, thundered*. The list goes on, and this is a fun activity to determine more word tags than merely *said*. A word of caution, however, *said* is a workable word for most writing; overdoing the synonyms for the sake of variety and not a reasonable purpose can create muddy writing. Don't overdo *said*, but don't go overboard with synonyms either.

When they have finished the drafts for the Oral History Project memoirs, they are ready to proofread and then turn them into final copy. The final copies are then published on the triptych. Students now experience writing for two audiences. They are compiling or writing the memoir to be viewed in the context of their Oral History project. The memoir then becomes a part of the whole product and process. However, the memoir is also intended for the subject, especially if written or presented by the student. And, the memoir is intended for a larger audience to read and comprehend another piece of the puzzle of the subject. Who is this person? What happened in her life? What influenced how this person turned out? All these questions and more form the questions of this much larger audience, and some of the answers can be found in other parts of the project.

CD Connection

Go to Main Menu and click on Gallery. Scroll down to Memoir Module, Video - Thoughts About the Value of the Memoir.

We all love stories. Stories have been one of our main means of educating people throughout history. Now we have added this element to the reconstruction of a person's life. The memoir, a piece of writing that relates how something influenced a person's life in some way, becomes the words and the experience of the subject speaking out from the project. Everything else on the project is essentially the subject seen through the lens of the student's perception, but this part is unique. The memoir is the time for the subject to give his voice to the project by documenting his uniquely personal story. In this telling of the story, the subject, the student, the teacher, and all who read the memoir share in experiencing the voice that has become a vibrant, vital part of the Oral History Project.

For more information on the memoir process:

Heard, Georgia. 1995. *Writing Toward Home: Tales and Lessons to Find Your Way*. Portsmouth, NH: Heinemann.
Ledeoux, Dennis. 1993. *Turning Memories into Memoirs: A Handbook for Writing Lifestories*. Lisbon Falls, ME: Soleil Press.
Roorbach, Bill. 1998. *Writing Life Stories: How to Make Memories into Memoirs, Ideas into Essays, and Life into Literature*. Cincinnati, OH: Story Press.

Appendix 5—A

Coconut Grove Fire Tragedy

By: Maggie Witmer

There have been many tragedies in the past. Some of us have been witnesses of them and others have only heard stories or saw it on the news. There was one tragedy that went down in history. It was said to be the worst nightclub fire disaster in history. My grandpa, Mike DeSisti, was in this disaster. It was known as the Coconut Grove Fire.

It was November 28, 1942. My grandpa was transferred to Harvard University to be an ensign for the Navy. It was in the winter and therefore he had on his heavy winter coat, hat, and gloves. The Coconut Grove was a fun nightclub where everyone would go and hang out. My grandpa was supposed to meet some of his friends there. So he walked into the club and through his eyes saw this beautiful girl. She was wearing an evening gown. She was on fire.

Everyone was panicking and rushed to the two revolving doors. Mike was pushed and shoved into the crowd. His hat and gloves fell off from the commotion and he was by the door. The door was stuck and no one could get out that way nor could they get in. Both doors were jammed with people stacked on top of each other. My grandpa lay unconscious while everything was happening.

Rescue workers came and got people out of the club. They didn't know if my grandpa was dead or alive. He had been burnt on his eyes and hands. They got him out through, and took him to the hospital. His coat saved his life.

Mike's parents were Italian. They did not speak English and they didn't have the news back then. They had no idea what had happened to their son, until there was a picture on the magazine LIFE. It was a picture of a hospital in Boston where there were

Appendix 5–A *continued*

lines of patients in beds from the fire. One of them was my grandpa. To see if it was true, one of Mike's relatives rushed up to Boston to see if it was him, and sure enough it was.

His sister, Lena, sent him flowers and Mike said the first thing he saw when he woke up was those flowers. My grandma went up to see him and when she did she didn't recognize him because of all the bandages. She walked up the aisle of beds and walked right past Mike. When she walked back through Mike reached his arm and she knew it was him.

It's amazing how we take our lives for granted. You never know what will happen in a second. 492 people were killed in this disaster. My grandfather has been through many tragedies in his life. But he has survived every single one. He is in good shape for everything he has been through and everyone in my family is very proud of him and looks up to him with envy. He is surely a hero in my heart.

Appendix 5–B Reflection Sheet

Chapter 5: Memoir

What is my response to the opening thoughts and questions (*in italics*)?

What was the most valuable information that I gained personally and/or for my classroom?

What do I still need to know more about? Where could I go to get that information?

What ideas can I add to what I've already learned?

6 Portrait

Figure 6–1 Junior high students practice using the digital camera.

Think about that album or box of pictures that your family has or look at the sports section of the newspaper. What do the photos tell you about the people who are depicted? What can you tell by the clothing they are wearing? Do they seem flamboyant or reserved? Does anything in the picture tell what was going on when the shot was taken? Can you tell the moods of members of your family or your friends on the day that the picture was taken?

A team of middle school teachers from an intercity school district attends a weeklong professional development session that centers on using oral history as a means to integrate the language arts. They leave the seminar determined to implement the model in their sixth-grade classroom. The district already had in place a requirement that students would complete a project at the end of each grade level. To date these projects have been mostly of the paper-and-pen variety. The teachers saw the Oral History Project as a way for students to engage in a meaningful experience that went beyond the traditional to a venture that would enable them not only to increase their skills in reading, writing, speaking, and listening but to learn more about themselves, their families, and their community.

Problems abounded.

As with many intercity schools, resources were very limited, parental support was nonexistent, and there had been enough "incidents" at the middle school that there were two full-time security police on campus at all times. As with many intercity schools, these teachers were experienced and dedicated educational professionals determined that their students would not have a truncated experience that is a variation on a theme but rather would have all that they needed to ensure a full, rich experience.

Using the district "chain of command" and community resources, the teachers were able to secure permission and the funds for materials. The last hurdle was the digital cameras for the portraits—and cameras it had to be! Finally, they were promised ten digital cameras at cost—hardly enough for the 120 sixth graders who would be involved in the Oral History Project. A plan was devised. Cameras would be hung on hooks outside of the principal's office. Students would check them out on a first-come, first-served basis for one night of use, returning them to their respective hooks in the morning. The teachers went before the school board to request the monies for the cameras. They received the reaction that they expected: the honor system was beyond the students; the cameras would be gone the first day; these students would steal them and use the money to buy drugs . . . ! However, the teachers prevailed and the funds for the cameras were approved. The project began and the cameras were available by midpoint in the process. Teachers had spent time explaining the importance of shared resources and the students and their families were so engrossed in the project and the end product that by the end of the project, nine of the cameras were still in place and functional—none had been stolen, but one had been dropped and broken—and returned to the school.

One could conjecture about why, in this instance, the expected behavior of the students did not occur. When asked why it worked, the teachers replied that this was the first time that there was a project that was the same for all the students at a grade level, that all students could complete no matter their ability level, where cooperation, not competition was the order of the day, and where the final product was to be shared schoolwide.

Though hours and hours of teacher and student time are put into the components of the Oral History Project, the portrait is usually the first thing that catches the viewer's eye when viewing a triptych. If a triptych is not the product, the portrait is often the centerpiece for other presentation styles, for example, the cover of a folio or scrapbook. The portrait delivers that first impression of the subject. It captures just one moment but expresses something important about that person. A good portrait reveals personality traits of the person and sometimes the person's artifacts or props are judiciously added to accomplish this. Because the person has already been interviewed, the student, as photographer, is thinking about the person's oral history, and more details than just a face become appropriate. It should never be just a head shot, but should reveal information about the subject that aids the viewer in an understanding of that person. At the same time, it should not be so cluttered with props and background that the subject is lost as the focus of the portrait.

Though the anecdote above discusses the digital camera as the instrument for obtaining a portrait, this is not the only way to do it. Resources are limited at most schools, be they urban, suburban, or rural, so cameras of any type may be beyond budgetary constraints. Student-rendered portraits using various media (oils, watercolor, charcoal, pencil, and so on) are equally acceptable and in the best-case scenario, instruction occurs in cooperation with the art or vocational education teacher.

As educators, we are quite accustomed to grading and scoring written work. We have designed and shared scoring guides and rubrics. We can reach consensus on the characteristics of writing and have multiple measures for ascertaining student's comprehension of materials that they have read. The same should apply to the portrait that is part of this project. This is not an add-on, but should be done thoughtfully with criteria for success that are clearly delineated and communicated to students.

Instruction

Students need to know that portraits are an art form that has particular characteristics and its own standards and criteria. They are the visual representation of individual people and are distinguished by the fact

CD Connection

Go to Main Menu and click on Gallery. Scroll down to the Portrait Module, Teacher Introduces The Portrait Assignment.

that these representations include references to the person's character, profession, age and/or interests. This is accomplished through the use of props and backgrounds. An exact replica is not always the goal; many artists alter the appearance of their subjects by embellishing their images to emphasize or minimize certain characteristics. Portraits can include only the head of the subject or they can depict the shoulders and head, the upper torso, or an entire figure either sitting or standing. Portraits can be executed in any medium including sculpted stone and wood, wax, painted ivory, pastel, carved cameos, and hammered or poured metals. At this point, the teacher will inform students of the accepted media for the Oral History Project. In most school settings portraits are drawn and painted or taken by camera. The emphasis in the following is on the use of the digital camera as its use necessitates a technology component that is an increasingly necessary curriculum requirement.

Also to be taught here is the different approach or relationship that the student must adopt with his subject at the point that the photographic portrait is to be taken. Presuming that the interview occurred before this point, the relationship has been one of inquiry and learning. The student approaches the interviewee as someone who is seeking the particular kind of information that the subject alone is able to provide. The preparation for the photo shoot requires interpersonal skill of a slightly different nature. Many people balk at having their picture taken or become self-conscious or embarrassed in a way that they don't when they are imparting information that they are confident and knowledgeable about. For the portrait, the student must build confidence and trust with the subject, helping them to feel comfortable with the shoot. Sometimes, just promising that a number of shots will be taken and that the subject can help choose the one that will be used diffuses the situation.

It may be helpful to solicit advice from more experienced teachers or from a professional photographer for this component of the Oral History project. Using cameras, digital or the more traditional ones, requires specific technological skills. Portraiture is often taught with the help of the art teacher. This may be the start of a wonderful collaboration and the arts teacher may welcome the chance to participate in a cooperative learning venture. Again, if the portraits are going to be photographs, a particular type of expertise is required, and many teachers have used a community resource person such as a local studio photographer or a photographer from the local newspaper. Be sure that the person is comfortable working with middle school students and has a very clear understanding of your requirements for the final product. Most people are delighted to share their knowledge and expertise.

That being said, you might want to deliver this instruction yourself because of time and scheduling restraints or your own developing interest in portraiture. There are many sites on the Internet that provide information about the basics of digital photography (Hewlett Packard, for example, offers a free six-week digital photography course complete with activities, assignments, and quizzes).

Students need to learn the basic components of the camera that they will be using. Depending on the camera used, they need to know the settings so that they can control light, focus and speed. They need to take a lot of practice photographs before they begin to take the shots that will be used to depict their subject. Testing the camera in a controlled situation and noting what they are doing, and how this is affecting the pictures that are being taken is a skill-building tool that leads to reducing the chances of losing special moments or special shots. In addition to time with the camera, students need to know some basics about photography; the following are an abbreviated version of the "top ten tips" used with permission from photographer, Jim Miotke, which can be found on his website: wwwbetterphoto.com/exploring/tips/asp; these tips reflect a consensus of advice for beginning photographers.

Top Ten Photo Tips

1. **Move in closer.**
Each time you spot a subject, snap a shot and then move in closer for a better shot. Having your subject almost fill the frame helps your viewer understand and appreciate your photo. Also, details are often more interesting than an overall view. Keep moving in closer until you are sure a 4 by 6-inch photo will successfully represent your subject (see Figure 6–2).

Photos by Sam Bidleman

Figure 6–2 Which photo best captures the subject?

2. **Be quick.**
If it is at all possible that your subject may stop smiling, bolt, or just get tired of waiting for you to take the picture, shoot once right away. Practice getting quicker and quicker to the draw. Do not worry so much about wasting film (with a digital, there isn't any and no darkroom chemicals, either) and do not wait until you're absolutely certain all the knobs and buttons are in their correct position. A good motto might be, "Shoot first, and ask questions later" (see Figure 6–3).

3. **Compose your work of art.**
Even if you don't plan on selling your photo to the Smithsonian, make an effort to keep it balanced and beautiful. On one level or another, everyone responds better to a picture that has all elements in balance or that leads the eye along an interesting path through the photo.

For starters:

- Keep the horizon level.
- Crop out extra elements that you are not interested in.
- Consciously place your subject where you think it most belongs rather than just accepting it wherever it happens to land in the photo.
- Play with perspective so that all lines show a pattern or lead the eye to your main subject.
- Work with the "rule of thirds," a technique used by photographers for a special effect whereby the field of vision is broken

Figure 6–3 Posed or spontaneous?

Figure 6–4 Which photo has better focus? Was the rule of "thirds" used?

down into three areas across and three areas down (for more information go to www.silverlight.co.uk/tutorial/compose_expose/thirds.html/ or use your computer search engine using the keywords, "rule of thirds"). See Figure 6–4.

Figure 6–5 Do both photos tell you the same things about the subject?

4. Be picky.
Discern what you are really interested in and center your efforts on getting the best photo of this person, their mood, culture, and so on. Be sure to keep anything that would distract out of the picture. The easiest way to do this is to watch your borders and recompose if something—such as an unattractive telephone wire, an old soda can, a distracting sign, or your finger—hangs into your picture. You can:

- focus in on a close-up that tells the whole story
- move around until you manage to make a neat pattern that leads to the subject, or
- take a panning shot so that, if you're successful, the subject remains in focus while the background goes blurry (See Figure 6–5)

5. Focus on your subject.
Practice shooting with different apertures and monitor the results to learn how depth-of-field effects your photo. You will find that a smaller depth-of-field (and smaller f-stop #) focuses all the attention upon your subject. See Figure 6–6.

6. Experiment in time
One of the most basic, overlooked, and fun aspects of photography is that you have the power to slow time down or catch a split second. One image happens so slowly that we could never see it and the other happens so quickly in real time that we would never notice it. Play with shutter speed! Use a slow shutter speed and a tripod to make a pretty picture of any person who stays in place. On the other hand,

Figure 6–6   What is the photographer's focus?

you can use a fast shutter speed (1/500 and up) to capture an object in motion. Combining a fast shutter speed with a long lens, you are able to catch the expression on your favorite running back's face as he slips past the final defense toward a winning touchdown. Remember, catching the moment in fast-paced action photography may take a little more practice so—hang in there.

7. Look at the light.

By this, I don't mean look into the sun; that won't do at all. But it is good to see what kind of light you are working with. Which way are the shadows falling? Unless you want a silhouette effect, where your subject is black against an interesting background, it's generally best to shoot with the sun behind you. How is the light affecting your subject? Is the subject squinting? Is the light blazing bright upon your whole subject? This works well if you are in love with the bold colors of your subject. Side lighting, on the other hand, can add drama but can also cause extreme, hard-to-print contrasts. Lastly, use indirect light to make your subject glow soft and pretty. See Figure 6–7.

8. Watch the weather, too.

Look outside and decide whether you are going to want to have the sky in your picture. If it's overcast, simply keep the sky out of your

Figure 6–7 Does lighting make a difference?

pictures as much as possible. This is usually the best way to avoid both muted tones in your subject and washed-out skies in your background. You might also find black-and-white pictures of an overcast day more pleasing than color.

9. Keep it simple.
While you may wish to have "all the bells and whistles" available just in case, you will probably get the best results if you do not try to use them all the time and instead learn a simple set-up that works best for you in most situations. For beginning photographers this may mean setting the camera on its automatic program.

10. Be bold.
Do not allow yourself to be paralyzed by fears about correct film, correct settings, or correct social policy. If you are afraid of upsetting someone by taking their picture, ask first (maybe before you finalize them as your oral history subject) if it's okay. Ask them to sign a release (see Appendix 6–A, Photographic Release Letter). Always, always get a release form that describes how you will use their portrait and do not go beyond that agreed upon use without getting additional permissions. Some people are very sensitive about being photographed before the fact, but are more than pleased when they see how it fits into the overall project.

In addition to practice with the camera, students need to see lots and lots of portraits, both conventional and nonconventional. Photographic examples from Ansel Adams or portraits from Picasso might identify both ends of a spectrum—from more formal "sittings" to cubist renderings. Bad photos—someone with what appears to be a light pole growing out of his head—will help them avoid the same kinds of mistakes in their own photos. Trips outside the classroom to local photographers or artists, a museum, or historical society will enable students to see a multiplicity of portrait examples.

Assessment

The criteria for the successful portrait must be established during and be embedded into the instructional phase. Students learn about and then begin to practice with the cameras: the criteria must be there from the beginning so that they know when they have met the established criteria. Though it may be tempting for assessment to be a

CD Connection

Go to Main Menu and click on Gallery. Scroll down to the Portrait Module, Assessing the Portrait. Go to Portrait Module and click on Products, Assessments, and Rubics.

question of "I like it; I don't like it," students need clear descriptors of all levels on the way to the successful product. Rubrics clarify for the students what must be included.

There is but one problem with this element of the oral history process: students love to take portraits and will very often not be satisfied with their results; they love to take picture after picture (and not always of their subject). It may be well to limit the number of total pictures to be taken or the time with the camera.

Though much time has been spent discussing camera techniques, photography is but one avenue to the portrait element of this Oral History Project. Cameras can be difficult to obtain and if they are not available to all students in an equitable manner, the project becomes tilted toward those with more financial means at their disposal. No matter how the project is put together and presented, it is imperative that all students have access to the same materials and that your assessments are based on what is provided for everyone. For example, if a student sets up a TV and VCR and shows a tape of his interview as part of his presentation, it may show that he has the ability to buy the necessary equipment to record an interview, but it is the quality of the interview, not the camcorder, that is to be assessed and scored here. Although most portraits will be photographs or drawings (see Figure 6–8), keep in mind that portraits can be rendered using various techniques and materials.

Choosing a form other than photography can serve to put the focus of the project on the oral history rather than on the equipment and this can be viewed as a positive, but so can learning to use a new piece of technology. Suffice it to say; the choice is yours and depends on your resources and the needs of your students.

For more information on how to do successful portraits:

Peterson, Bryan. 2004. *Understanding Exposure: How to Shoot Great Photographs with a Film or Digital Camera (Updated Edition)*. New York: Amphoto Books, Watson-Guptill Publications.
Story, Derrick. 2005. *Digital Photography Pocket Guide, Third Edition* Sebastopol, CA: O'Reilly Digital Studio.

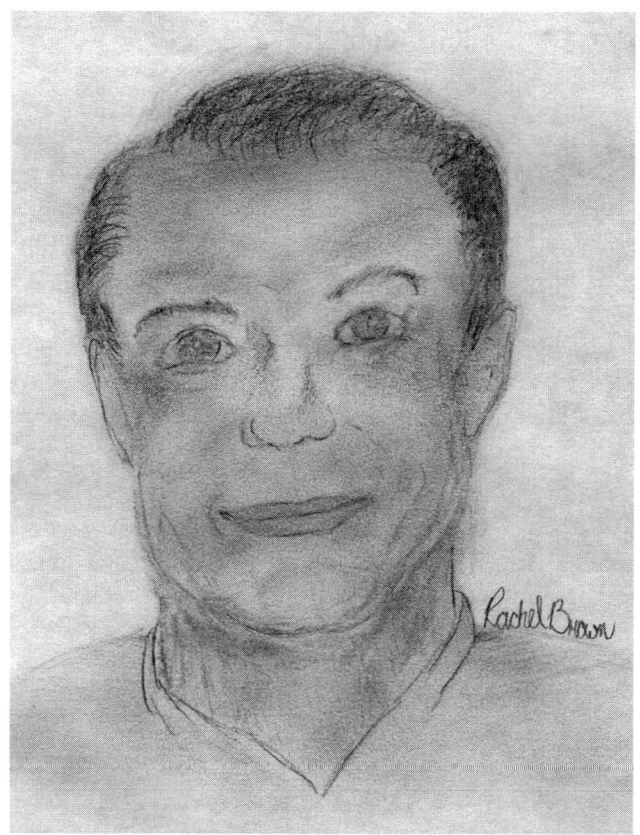

Figure 6–8 A photographic portrait has been used to create this artistic rendering.

Appendix 6—A Photographic Release Letter

I hereby grant to author or publisher, and their respective licensees, successors, and assigns, the right and permission, with respect to those photographs taken of me or the minor named below on whose behalf I am signing, and with respect to any printed matter in connection therewith, to do the following:

1. To include such photographs in all editions of the book tentatively entitled *The Oral History Project* and/or on its book cover, in all media, and in the advertising, publicity, and promotion thereof.

2. To use my name or the name of the minor on whose behalf I am signing, in connection with the foregoing.

I hereby release, discharge and agree to indemnify and hold harmless the author or publisher and their respective heirs, legal representatives, licensees, successor, and assigns, from all claims and demands whatsoever arising out of or in connection with the foregoing, and waive any right to inspect or approve the same.

_____

Signature of Subject of Photograph

_____

Printed Name and Address

I hereby certify that I am the parent and/or guardian of _____, a minor under the age of eighteen years, and hereby consent on behalf of said minor to the use of any of the photographs taken of said minor pursuant to the terms set forth in this Photographic Release, including, without limitation, the release, discharge, and hold harmless provisions thereof.

_____

Signature of Parent or Guardian of Minor Subject of Photograph

_____

Printed Name and Address

Appendix 6–B Reflection Sheet

Chapter 6: Portrait

What is my response to the opening thoughts and questions (*in italics*)?

What was the most valuable information that I gained personally and/or for my classroom?

What do I still need to know more about? Where could I go to get that information?

What ideas can I add to what I've already learned?

7 Presentation

Figure 7–1 Teacher Jamilla Rice presents the Oral History of Victoria Donati.

Think about a time when you had to speak in front of your class or another group. What was the occasion? What helped you to prepare? What do you think was successful? What could be improved? Most importantly, how did you feel?

Think about all the work that your students have put into the various components of your Oral History Project: the hours spent on choosing a subject, preparing to conduct an interview, the time spent with the subject, using a writing process to create a memoir and a feature article, choosing a significant artifact, collecting information, conducting research, and the thought and caring that went into the portrait. They are almost there! The last step is to assemble all that they have gathered and present it in a manner that truly captures the essence of the person they have interacted with.

Their time is limited. What are the most important things that they want to tell their audience about the person that they studied? What were the most enjoyable and the most challenging aspects of the process? How has this project affected them personally and academically? What is it that they want the viewer to pay attention to as they peruse the project?

A small town at the northern border of the state . . . population: five-thousand, eighth-grade enrollment: 180. An early spring evening and for the sixth consecutive year, there is an "event" in the school gym at 7:30. Invitations have been sent to community members, to town officials, to the Secretary of Education, and to other staff of the State Department of Education.

Cars begin to fill the parking lot as early as 6:00. Attendees range in age from infants-in-arms to octogenarians. By 7:15, the Harlan Rowe Junior High School Band is in full swing and the gym is filled to capacity.

The event? The Athens Area School District eighth-grade Oral History Fair! This is the culmination of a months-long project for all students at this grade level, using the seven components of the Oral History Project the model described in the preceeding chapters.

Just as the components of an Oral History Project vary depending on the circumstances/constraints found at a particular district or building, so do the ways in which products are presented. This is probably the easiest component to skip, but its value is immeasurable in terms of the students' learning and having a wide-ranging, standards-based experience. Most states have speaking and listening standards, but when teachers are asked how they assess speaking, they usually have students do formal speeches on a teacher-chosen topic. Assessment of listening is the weakest of all assessments for standards. The presentation of students' Oral History Projects provides opportunities for student-driven, rather than teacher-driven, oral presentations. It is also an excellent opportunity to introduce and to refine listening skills both from a courtesy and skills perspective.

Planning for the Presentation

Advocates of backward planning or "teaching with the end in mind" start their planning by asking themselves what the most effective venue for sharing the end product would be. How and where it will be presented also determine the form of the final product. It does not have to be as wide ranging or extensive as those cited in previous chapters, but just as the writing process has publishing as the final step, the Oral History Project most often includes group sharing as its publishing step. Presentations can be formal or informal based on whether they are to be delivered in the classroom or some other setting such as, an in- or out-of-school assembly, a retirement home, or some other setting off campus.

Choosing Formal or Informal Presentation Mode

As a first step, discuss the setting in which the presentation will be made and what will be expected of the student. Model a presentation by presenting a triptych—the one that they made, the one made about them or one completed by a student in a previous year. (See Figure 7–2 and 7–3.)

Triptychs are pictured here and are discussed throughout this text. Those that are shown here were purchased from an office supply store and are made of cardboard that is scored to fold into three sections with the middle section as the widest. This enables them to stand without being propped. They are available in a range of colors. The students were also provided with a variety of arts and crafts materials, but many of them provided or created their own decorations. Some triptychs not shown here have been made by cutting up boxes.

Figure 7–2   Students displaying their triptychs.

Figure 7–3 Students creating their triptychs.

Figure 7–4 A student formally presents the information on her triptych.

Also, triptychs are not the only vehicle for presenting the project—albums, wall displays, dioramas, and other types of poster board also serve the purpose. The goal is to display the writing pieces, artifacts, and research results so that they can be read and viewed by the audience. The presentation examples on the CD-ROM can also be shown to students as further examples.

If the formal presentation is chosen, the teacher can then discuss important points to think about when making a presentation. These might include things such as:

- Know your speaking environment and your audience.
    Will a microphone be necessary?
    Will there be a chance to practice with it?

What is the age of the audience?
Are they there voluntarily or because they have to be there?
- Have a structure, purpose, and learning points for the presentation.
  What is the time limit for the formal presentation?
  What are the main points to be addressed, and in what order?
  Do I concentrate on the subject, the process, or both?
  What is the main thing I want my audience to learn?
- Acknowledge the importance of preparation and practice.
  Have I gone over my material so that I do not have to read entirely from notes?
  Have I listened to my classmates' presentations and have they listened to mine?
  Has the teacher modeled a good presentation?
- Consider the characteristics of good nonverbal communication such as eye contact, good posture, and natural gestures.
  Am I prepared to scan the audience and make eye contact with them instead of talking to my project with my back to my audience?
  Am I confident enough (because I've practiced) to stand tall and not slouch with my hands in my pockets.
  Do I effectively use my hands and facial expressions to convey positive attitudes about my subject and the process?
- Consider the characteristics of good verbal communication such as avoiding slang and clichés.
  Am I using a "universal" language that can be understood by everyone listening?
  Am I careful to define terms that may not be understood by all (scientific, artistic, generational terms)?

With these considerations in mind, the teacher can develop a set of criteria with his or her students that will be used to assess the formal presentation (see Appendix 7–A, Presentation Tools for Implementation).

Less formal presentations still need criteria on which to be judged, not unlike the ones above. Whether the presentation is formal or informal depends on the audience and the setting. If the format is the Oral History Fair mentioned in the anecdote at the beginning of the chapter, a formal presentation is neither practical nor effective. In an auditorium with over a hundred students and their triptychs, students talk about their projects as people pass by to view them. Although there are established criteria and students have given thought to the points that they will emphasize, a great deal of what they say is determined by questions from those who are viewing their triptychs (Figure 7–5).

A Presentation Continuum

There are many ways to "package" and present the Oral History Project. Though this text is targeted for those who teach at the middle school or junior high school level, the following provides context and, perhaps, a few ideas about how presentation models can work with your students or can be modified so that students of all abilities can participate (see also Appendix 7-B, Oral History Components Timeline).

CD Connection

Go to Main Menu and click on Gallery. Scroll down to the Presentation Module, Teacher Describes How He Modeled The Presentation for His Class.

An Example at the Introductory Level
Students are asked to interview their grandparents or another older person to find out what games they played when they were young and how these games were the same or different from the games that children play today. The final product was to depict one game that was the same and one game that was different. The children were to involve their parents and to use either photographs or drawings for their comparisons. This was not meant to be an independent project for the children. Its purpose was at least twofold: To have students use games to find out how their childhood was the same or different from those who are removed by a generation or two and to involve

Figure 7–5 A student ready to talk about his project.

parents in this learning. (Note: Not all children have access to grandparents, so choosing a subject can be problematic. Alternatives might be to ask the students to find someone who is at least thirty years older than they are, to use staff of the school [teachers, office staff, janitors, cafeteria workers], or to use churches, synagogues, or mosques for recruiting subjects of the appropriate age.)

Participation was voluntary and the parental involvement in putting the project together varied widely. The culminating event was a sleepover in the school gym during which students and parents shared their products. These varied from a detailed playground diorama complete with jungle gym to simple drawings of trees with heads cut from present day photos of Nana and granddaughter pasted to the limbs. Presentation criteria were simple, with the children telling things that were the same and different. The most emotional response was from parents who searched through old photos that they hadn't viewed in years and shared family stories, many for the first time. Though the parent sharing had not been planned, parents were profuse in their appreciation of the opportunity to talk about family history with their children and edified that the children were inquisitive and interested.

The first year only six students showed; by year three, word had spread and twice that number or two thirds of the students, were attending with their parents. Soon grandparents and other subjects began to ask if they too, could attend.

An Example at the Novice Level

Projects at this level can be accomplished individually or with a partner. The feature article and the photograph are either eliminated or reconfigured. Students can write a simple memoir using teacher-created questions such as where the students were born, their first memory, their favorite toy, and so on. Interview questions can be configured so that written answers can be edited into a piece written about the interviewee that is not a feature article per se. Student drawings can be substituted for photographs and, of course, this is possible at all levels. In some schools, the art teacher is involved and this work is done in his class. Triptychs are but one way to assemble the products of the process. Scrapbooks, poster board, or construction paper are also suitable.

One model for this process is to pair young students with those who are the oldest in the building. These students can be the subjects of the project, or they can serve as mentors or aides to the younger student. They can be the photographer if they are not the subjects, help with the assembly of the final product and work with the younger students to prepare for the oral presentation. This necessitates the cooperation of central office and the upper-grade teachers so that the students from the two grade levels can have time to spend with each other during the school day. The rubric for the finished product has to be shared with the older student. They should have a rubric that describes levels of achievement on their part and some academic credit or reward should be in place so that the older students have an answer to "What's in it for me?" As with most innovations, the most hurdles occur during the first year. The event eventually shifts to something the older students look forward to as part of what happens their last year at an organizational or building level. One building did the mentor model for three years and the meetings between the students occurred in January, with presentations occurring in the late spring. Because an inordinate number of snow days wreaked havoc with the school calendar, they decided not to implement the mentor model during the fourth year. The outcry from students ("not fair") and the parents of the upper-grade students ("this was the first time my daughter really took responsibility for something and saw it through to completion") was sufficient to have it restored for the fifth year.

Possible Components for "Older" Student Rubric

Offered in Figure 7–6 is a "starter" rubric. It is meant to give a model and to be modified to include components that are particular to a selected Oral History Project. You may want to add or delete components. Note the tips for writing rubrics at the end.

At the Intermediate Level

Students at this level are capable of doing all the components of the Oral History Project as described in previous chapters. Decide before you begin, based on the constraints of time, money and administrative support (or lack thereof), what the scope of your project will be.

CD Connection

Go to Main Menu and click on Presentation. Go to Products, Assessments, and Rubrics across the top tab.

What is the nature of the final presentation?

Will you use triptychs or some other material?

Where will it be held?

Component	4	3	2	1
Involvement	Respectively and attentively listens to the student's ideas and helps the student to carry them out. Is the "enthusiastic guide on the side."	Listens to the student's ideas. Helps the student execute them.	Tells the Student what to do.	Does all the work for the student.
Responsibility	Meets with the student over and above the required time. Makes contact with the student to make sure that s/he is up to date.	Meets with the student at all the required times.	Is often absent at the required scheduled times or has some excuse for not being in attendance.	May or may not be present at the requested times, and is uninvolved and nonresponsive to the younger student.
Interaction with younger student	Try writing this component on your own.	Tip: Avoid words that are subjective, e.g., "beautiful," "easy," "several," etc.	Tip: Make sure that there are four distinct descriptions of minimal to advanced so that scoring is not confusing.	Tip: Don't quantify—three meetings are not always better than two meetings that are well planned and executed.
Add components as you see fit				

Figure 7–6 Sample of possible components for "older" students rubric.

Who will be invited?

Will it be combined with some other school or community event?

Should it be advertised?

Is it classroom based and maybe just shared with other classes at the same level or will you seek a wider audience?

Figure 7–7   The Oral History Project helps students connect across generations.

Buying triptychs for a whole class can be expensive; in some cases parents can afford to buy them for their children, or the district can supply them. In other cases, this is not even a remote possibility. Be creative in using other materials. One teacher spent several months asking appliance and furniture stores to save their big boxes for her. She took them home and cut them into panels that she joined with masking tape to make triptychs. As the personnel of the stores attended presentations by their children and learned what the boxes were being used for, she soon found them cut and assembled when she arrived to pick them up (Figure 7–7).

The special appeal of this Oral History Project is that it does not exclude any student on the grounds of ability and it can be a whole-class experience. All students can complete the components; the quality will vary from basic to sophisticated. If the intergenerational model is chosen, parameters can be set—for example, the subject has to be at least 40 years older than the student—assuring that no one is left out because they do not have an accessible grandparent. With families increasingly mobile and with people of all ages availing themselves of email and other technological advances, students are beginning to communicate and complete their Oral History Projects with grandparents that they may see only a few times a year.

At the Middle School and Junior and Senior High Level

Though seven components of the Oral History Project are described in this book, teachers have added or subtracted from this set. The model most often described here is the intergenerational one, but there are other models. Students can focus on a particular profession. Students interview carpenters, doctors, steelworkers, or any other profession of their choice to learn about the preparation for these careers and the resultant lifestyle. This can easily be integrated into a careers or vocational course. When completed and presented, students will have extensive information on a wide range of occupations. When the focus of the project shifts, it often results in some changes to the components of the project. Perhaps the written pieces will be a research piece on the profession rather than the feature article. If asking perfect strangers to write a memoir seems presumptuous, they might be interviewed about how they came to choose their careers and the information gathered into a "memoir" that is written by the student rather than the subject. Another idea is to develop a time line for becoming a (carpenter or steelworker) that could also serve as a substitute for the feature article.

Teachers have chosen important figures in history and the students wrote the memoir in the first person based on their research of the historical character. The feature article was written in the prose appropriate to the time and place in which the character lived. When the focus changes, the components have to be revisited and sometimes altered.

Artifacts can be created based on what is known about how the subject influenced history and what was appropriate for the era—a present-day bird feather to represent the quill used to sign the Declaration of Independence might be one example, or rather than a feature article, an obituary of Benjamin Franklin written in the style, voice and tone of *Poor Richard's Almanac*.

Development of specific topics (women's movement), political parties (Whigs), science (pasteurization), social studies (importance of harbors in America's cities) serves to have students in control of their own learning and away from essays on topics chosen from a predetermined list. This does not mean that there are not well-defined teacher-determined criteria that have to be articulated to students, but that students are encouraged to go beyond just the facts to personal interaction with people who were or are involved in the topics, gathering relevant background information is not done in a vacuum but connects to an individual that they are developing a personal relationship with and who has intimate involvement in the area to be researched. As students become more and more involved in their topic or subject they tend to enhance their presentation on their own as demonstrated by the fact that more and more students are adding lighting, audio and computer PowerPoint® to their presentations, not because it was a requirement, not just because the student was aware of audience and what would draw people to their product, but because history has become alive and real, not just something that appears in text. Students are motivated to go beyond what is required and to become the catalyst for their own learning. Soon some students are complaining that the triptych is too small, or the scrapbook has too few pages, because they have all this "stuff" that they want to share.

The writing of the rubric becomes essential for this scenario. If a four-point rubric is used to score the final product, a score of four is only awarded to those who have gone well beyond the teacher-established criteria. Unlike many other academic projects, you will have many potential fours.

The first year of implementation, many districts are not able to fiscally support a huge event such as an Oral History Fair, complete with refreshments, which necessitates staff being at the school after hours. Start small doing presentations either in your classroom, the library, or at your grade level. Gradually expand to an event that includes the subjects who were studied. Hold the event during school hours and have refreshment supplied voluntarily by the students. Your first evening event might be in conjunction with a PTA meeting or some other activity that is already on the school calendar. If you enjoy a success and you do something like an Oral History Fair or get covered by the local media, funding may become available in subsequent years.

As teachers use this model, they will mold it to their own and their students' needs. How will you do this *and* still teach all that you did in previous years?

Think Integration

Students today read, write, speak, and listen across their curriculum—switch some of that instructional and practice time into oral history–themed activities. In one school district the Oral History Project is everyone's job. It originated with the English teacher and he still includes the writing components in his curriculum, but he has gradually recruited the art teacher for implementing the portrait component and the computer teachers and the librarian for research. Each student has a double activity period once each six-day cycle. For a four-week period, all teachers in every activity period help students with their project, from encouraging them to stay on the time line to helping with writing and research ideas and assisting with the presentations. The entire middle school staff has a stake in successful completion by all students.

Think Sharing the Load

Recruiting other teachers makes the Oral History Project an example of cross-curricular work. Perhaps the art teacher could include the portrait in her curriculum. Other staff can be involved and/or be responsible for a component of the whole. The benefit is that the workload is shared and coverage becomes less of an issue. Teachers across a grade level are involved, and students have an enhanced sense of the importance of the endeavor. In many schools students experience no integration of subject matter; they are "victims" of the fragmented curriculum. They need to see cooperation among their teachers that moves everyone toward a common goal. The project that involves staff across a grade level is an excellent way for students to see a cooperative, collaborative model of both teaching and learning.

Think Paperless Model

In districts where technology is integral to the curriculum, students have loaded all components onto an Oral History website along with spoken narratives for each component (for example, www.patchworkhistory.com includes students "electronic" compilation of oral histories in and around Columbia County in Pennsylvania). Listening skills are demonstrated by students who view the presentation and when finished return to the classroom to answer three to five questions for each of the four presentations that they viewed and listened to on the website. In one school, this project is completed at the nineth-grade level. Components are taught by teachers in the classroom. In addition, each student receives a tenth-grade student mentor. The mentor has already completed the project and knows the anxiety that occurs at the beginning of the assignment and the pride in the final product. This is considered a huge plus for everyone involved: the ninth and tenth graders, and the faculty. Students who have completed the project look forward to being mentors the following year.

By their very nature, the projects described in this book outline a process that is truly authentic. The process and procedures that make up an Oral History Project use structures that are interactive, language- and meaning-based, and reflective. The formats require experiences that lead to lifelong habits of literacy and strongly influence and provide a template for future student work. With the presentation to a specific audience being the culminating activity, awareness of audience, self-direction, accountability, creative and critical thinking, not just regurgitation of factoids, are the essential components of a successful project.

The process of compiling oral histories described in this book is not just theoretical; it is based on the experiences of thousands of teachers, students, and community members coming together to celebrate themselves, their history, and most importantly, their stories. The schools and communities that they come from are representative of all strata of race, religion, and income. The students who participated were of differing abilities—from those with learning difficulties to the gifted. The teachers involved ranged from classroom aids to student teachers to those with doctorates. This process does not discriminate; it transforms. It is a can-do project for all students. Few students can go through it without being changed and enhanced. A measure of this is found within at the Oral History Fair anecdote cited at the beginning of this chapter, there is never a triptych, no matter what its quality, left behind to be discarded by the janitorial staff. (See Appendix 7–C, Themes and Habits for Literacy and the Oral History Project).

The intent of this project was to find an interesting, engaging *process* for integrating reading, writing, speaking, and listening. It became so much more. Because it is true that everyone has a story, a large group of people now have a written record of their lives and times; their stories will survive when they are gone. Because we treasure the individual differences that our students bring to us, we now have a way for all children to succeed.

A personal oral history: a treasure from the past, a gift for the present, and a legacy for the future.

For more information on presentations, go to:

Ritchie, Donald A. 1995. *Doing Oral History.* New York: Twayne.

Appendix 7–A   Presentation Tools for Implementation

1. **Timeline for teacher(s)**
    - Presentation—when, where, to whom (why them?), for the purpose of _____.
    - Beginning and end dates.
    - Other staff to be involved? How will I enlist them?
    - Dues dates by component and final product.
    - Instructional time involved and when.
    - Enhancements/adjustments for students at both ends of the learning spectrum.
    - Completed in school or, given my students, can some of this be homework, if so, what part(s)?
    - What will easily be accomplished given my "givens."
    - What will be difficult and what strategies will I use to ease the way? For example, is money a problem for me or for my students? What about "coverage"? How do I work this into my existing curriculum and not have it become an "add-on"?

2. **Timeline for students**
    - What is due? When is it due? How will it be graded—separately, or will I get one grade for the whole project? Will I have a role in determining the rubric or is it supplied?
    - Who will help me when I "hit the wall"?—by component.
    - Checklist of subtasks: e.g., getting ready to interview; learning to interview, practicing with classmate, choosing the subject to be interviewed, making the appointment, what to take with you to the interview, need a second session, etc.
    - Writing up the interview—is it graded separately or as a part of the final product?
    - Where on the triptych?

Appendix 7–B   Oral History Components Timeline

1. Interview
   Do I know the criteria for success?
   - Choose subject by _____.
   - Set up interview by _____.
   - Conduct first interview by _____.
   - Conduct second interview, if necessary, by _____.
   - Secure use of tape player/video by _____.
   - Transcribe notes by _____.
2. Memoir
   Do I know the criteria for success?
   - Will it be written by subject or by student?
   - In final form to be submitted on _____.
   - Revisions due by _____.
3. Research
   Do I know the criteria for success?
   - What are the sources?
     - Library?
     - Internet?
     - Historical society?
     - Primary sources?
     - Secondary sources?
     - How will they be cited on the final product?
4. Feature article
   Do I know the criteria for success?
   - To be completed and submitted by _____.
   - Revisions due by _____.
5. Portrait
   Do I know the criteria for success?
   - What is the medium (drawing, sculpture, photo, or other)?
   - Schedule sitting with subject
   - In final form, ready to post by _____
6. Presentation
   Do I know the criteria for success?
   - When will I give it?
   - Who will the audience be?
   - Will it be formal or informal?
   - Have I organized my thoughts?
   - Have I practiced it?

Appendix 7–C. Themes and Habits for Literacy and the Oral History Process

1. Literacy development—a lifetime endeavor.
   - Begins with the oral tradition
   - Includes everyone
2. Habits of Literacy
   - Self-directed
   - Self-managed
   - Self-assessed
3. Language strategies for proficiency
   - Scaffolding for processing, sharing, reflection, questioning
   - Investigating, explaining, doubting
   - Debating and becoming articulate
4. Creative thinking and problem solving
   - Identifies a problem
   - "Thinks outside the box"
   - Visualizes in new ways
   - Generates multiple solutions
5. Critical reflection and the development of expertise
   - Metacognition (reflection on my own learning)
   - Evaluation of multiple texts and media
6. Learning from and with others
   - Participate in conversations as both speaker and listener
   - Multiple perspectives and diverse learners
   - Importance of contest
   - Collaborative and cooperative group skills to meet goals
7. Using technology
   - To deepen understanding
   - To use visualization for understanding
   - To create new knowledge
   - To enter new environments for learning
   - To represent their learning using multimedia tools

Aligns with Grant Wiggins and Jay McTighe's *Understanding by Design* (1998), Robert Marzano's. *A Different Kind of Classroom: Teaching with Dimensions of Learning* (1992), and Carol Ann Tomlinson's *The Differentiated Classroom: Responding to the Needs of All Students* (1999).

Appendix 7–B Reflection Sheet

Chapter 6: Presentation

What is my response to the opening thoughts and questions (*in italics*)?

What was the most valuable information that I gained personally and/or for my classroom?

What do I still need to know more about? Where could I go to get that information?

What ideas can I add to what I've already learned?

Martin Jr., Bill and John Archambault. 1966. *Knots on a Counting Rope*. New York: Banton Doubleday Dell.

Miele, Joseph. The East Stroudsburg University *Weekly Professor.* "Is it Harder for Older People to Learn?" Pocono Record, February 28, 2002.

Perks, Robert, and Alistair Thomson. 1998. *The Oral History Reader*. London: Routledge.

Poorman, Linda, and Mary Wright. 2002. "Middle School Students Learning to Research: An Inquiry-Based Approach," in Maureen McLaughlin and MaryEllen Vogt *Creativity and Innovation in Content Area Teaching*. Norwood, MA: Christopher-Gordon Publishers, Inc.

Ritchie, Donald A. 1995. *Doing Oral History*. New York: Twayne Publishers.

Simmons, Elizabeth R. 1990. *Students Worlds, Students Words: Teaching Writing Through Folklore*. Portsmouth, NH: Boynton/ Cook Publishers.

Strickland, Dorothy, and Lesley Mandel Morrow (editors). 2000. *Beginning Reading and Writing*. New York: Teachers College Press.

Tomlinson, Carol Ann. 1999. *The Differentiated Classroom: Responding to the Needs of All Students*. Alexandria, VA: Association for Supervision and Curriculum Development.

Wiggins, Grant, and Jay McTighe. 1998. *Understanding by Design*. Alexandria, VA: Association for Supervision and Curriculum Development.

Zinsser, William. 1998. *Inventing the Truth*. New York: First Mariner Books.

```
LB1581 .O73 2006
The oral history project :
connecting students to thier
community, grades 4-8
```

Bibliography

Colonial Alliance for Public Schools. 2001. 6th Annual Excellence in Education Awards. Easton, PA: Colonial Intermediate Unit 20.

Dugan, Marion, Diane Dickson, Dick Heyler, Linda Reilly, Stephanie Romano, and Jean Winsand. 2002. The Oral History Project: Grades K–16. CD-Rom. BCD Interactive Study.

Dunaway, David K., and Willa K. Baum. 1984. *Oral History: An Interdisciplinary Anthology.* Nashville, TN: American Association for State and Local History.

Galda, Lee and Bernice Cullinan. 2000. "Reading Aloud from Culturally Diverse Literature" in Dorothy Strickland and Lesley Mandel Morrow (editors). *Beginning Reading and Writing.* New York: Teachers College Press.

Graves, Donald H. 1999. *Bring Life into Learning: Create a Lasting Literacy.* Portsmouth, NH: Heinemann.

Grushka, Kath, Julie Hinde-McLeod, and Ruth Reynolds. 2004. Reflective Practice in Teacher Education: Theory and Practice in One Australian University. Paper presented at the Reflective Practice Conference, June 23-25, 2004, Gloucester, UK.

Hoopes, James. 1979. *Oral History: An Introduction for Students.* Chapel Hill, NC: The University of North Carolina Press.

Kniffel, Leonard. 2005. "Listening as an Act of Love." *American Libraries: The Magazine of the American Library Association,* December.

Lattimer, Heather. 2003. *Thinking Through Genre: Units of Study in Reading and Writing Workshops 4–12.* Portland, ME: Stenhouse Publishers.

Lawlor, Veronica. 1995. *I Was Dreaming to Come to America: Memories from the Ellis Island Oral History Project.* New York: Viking.

Ledoux, Denis. 1993. *Turning Memories into Memoirs: A Handbook for Writing Lifestories.* Lisbon Falls, ME: Soleil Press.

Library of Congress. www.loc.gov/americaslibrary.

Marzano, Robert J. 1992. *A Different Kind of Classroom: Teaching with Dimensions of Learning.* Alexandria, VA: Association for Supervision and Curriculum Development.